Listening In

Listening In

Children Talk About Books
(and other things)

Thomas Newkirk
University of New Hampshire

with

Patricia McLure
Mast Way School
Lee, New Hampshire

Heinemann
Portsmouth, NH

1992

Heinemann Educational Books, Inc.

361 Hanover Street   Portsmouth, NH 03801-3959
Offices and agents throughout the world

Library of Congress Cataloging-in-Publication Data
Newkirk, Thomas.
     Listening in : children talk about books (and other things) / Thomas Newkirk with Patricia McLure.
         p.   cm.
     Includes bibliographical references (p.   ).
     ISBN 0–435–08713–4
     1. Language arts (Elementary)—United States. 2. Children—United States—Books and reading. 3. Children—United States—Language. 4. Communication in education—United States. I. McLure, Patricia. II. Title.
     LB1575.8.N38   1992
     372.6—dc20

91-38518
CIP

Designed by Jenny Jensen Greenleaf.
Front cover drawing by Sophie Feintuch.
Back cover drawing by Emma Tobin.
Printed in the United States of America.
92 93 94 95 96   9 8 7 6 5 4 3 2 1

To Beth, Sarah, Abby, Andy,
and Jessie (the dog)

Before I spoke with people, I did not think of all those things because there was no one to think them for. Now things come out of my mouth which are true.

MERRICK in *The Elephant Man*
by Bernard Pomerance

Contents

Acknowledgments

EVERY "I" IS, of course, a disguised "we." Every book is a chorus of voices, orchestrated (but not always invented) by the "I." Some of these voices are onstage, quoted and identified; others are offstage, those of editors and readers who helped shape the book. And, further off stage, there are the voices of what Vera John-Steiner calls "distant teachers"—scholars and writers who have, without knowing it, contributed to the book.

Among those on the stage, I want to thank first Pat McLure, who allowed me to tape her book discussion groups so extensively. She was extraordinarily generous with her time but more significantly with her commentary on the discussions. Week after week, she read through the transcripts and helped me hear what she heard.

The other main onstage voices are those of the students in her classroom. I want to thank them and their parents for allowing me to record their words. I have followed the convention of using pseudonyms for all the children, although with a pang of misgiving, for they essentially created the text—the set of transcripts— from which I drew. As I played and replayed (and replayed) the tapes, I came to see the special contributions their culture brought to the reading groups.

This project was made possible by the kind permission of John Lowy, principal of Mast Way School, who gave his encouraging support. The University of New Hampshire granted me a sabbatical that I used to write the book. For that time (and a thousand other favors), I want to thank Mike DePorte, chair of the English department, and Dean Stuart Palmer.

It was again an instructive pleasure to work with the editorial staff at Heinemann. George Bernard Shaw once wrote that "a first-rate editor is a rare bird indeed: two or three to a generation, in contrast to a swarm of authors, is as much as we get." I had the benefit of several first-rate editors. Philippa Stratton supported the book project when all I had to show her was a few transcripts. I want to thank Toby Gordon for her enthusiasm and editorial insight; I especially want to thank her for insisting that I deal with a couple of problem chapters when I was quite ready to be finished. I also benefited from a careful reading by Michael Ginsberg (he, too, convinced me that I wasn't finished). The production staff of Heinemann is equally a pleasure to work with. I want to thank Donna Bouvier and Alan Huisman for their attention to detail and their willingness to listen to authors' ideas for book design. And, at long last, I want to thank Sarah St. Onge, who copyedited both *More than Stories* and *Listening In.*

In writing this book, I tried to focus on Pat's classroom and on the children's talk, and I tried to tell the story as directly as I could. Consequently, the book is not heavily referenced, and even work that was crucial in the writing is not cited frequently. I have not, for example, cited the work on talk done in England in the 1970s, particularly Douglas Barnes's *From Communication to Curriculum* and James Britton's *Language and Learning,* both formative works for me. Courtney Cazden's work on classroom discourse has also been centrally important. I remember wandering into the Harvard Coop in 1972 and picking up *The Functions of Language in the Classroom,* a book I still keep within arm's reach. Her recent book *Classroom Discourse* summarized a wealth of studies that point to the issue that *Listening In* addresses—the restrictive sense of topicality in classrooms. The work of Gordon Wells, Anne Dyson, and Vivian Paley also helped shape my observations.

My own children will no doubt find some irony in the title of this book, for they often claim I am a poor listener, particularly when I'm in what they call "the uh-huh mode."

"Dad, I'd like a bike."

"Uh-huh."

"It's a mountain bike. At Bicycle Bob's. I really want it, Dad."

"Uh-huh."

"Can we get it before school? I really need it before school starts."

"Uh-huh."

Then, a couple of weeks later. "Dad, can we go get the bike you promised me?"

"What bike? I never promised you a bike!"

My children would tell you that I'm not the listener I appear to be in these pages. But, in my defense, I sometimes do pay attention to them, and their storytelling, kidding, and joking helped create the interest that led to this book. So it is to this disorderly family of mine, Beth, Sarah, Abby, Andy, and Jessie, that I dedicate this book.

1

A Better Mousetrap

THIS IS A book about staying on track. Or getting off track. Or trying to tell which is which. It is about talk that leaps unpredictably to new topics. It is about the movement of memory, and it is about the way open discussion kindles associated memories. It is also about the teacher who is often left in the dust ("How is that connected?"). We might as well begin with mousetraps.

Four readers in Pat McLure's first/second-grade class had gathered around the central table to share their books, as they always did at 9:30. Phillip shares *Newsman Ned Meets the New Family* (Kroll, 1988), and the discussion veers to mousetraps. People in the story had mistaken the new family's stuffed animals for the trunk of a circus elephant, which reminds Phillip of the problems he has had with the stuffing coming out of his koala bear, which reminds Susan of trouble with her stuffed white bear.

Susan: I had this big white bear—about that big—and I still have it but it's upstairs in the attic, and I know mice like eating it except they put the mice in a trap and close it.

Phillip: My father got these things like that you put on the ground and when the mice eat them they're supposed to die. But they haven't died. They just spitted it out and there was gook all over the place. So we got these glue traps. Glue traps work. My father got one but its feet stuck in the trap.

Pat [laughing]: I don't know about those glue traps.

Jed: What do you do with them if you ever get them out, though?

Phillip: My father throws them away.

Jed: I like the cheese traps. I checked one of them before, and the mouse was still alive.

Susan: My mother's boss, she has these glue traps and catches them by the tail and then I guess she pulls them out because it really hurts the mice and then she cuts off their tails and throws the mice in a pile and throws the tails in another pile.

Talk like this can pose a problem for the teacher. Is it relevant to the topic—in this case, *Newsman Ned Meets the New Family*? Should Pat edge the discussion back to the book? If so, how can she corral the talk without sapping the enthusiasm of the group?

If we are willing to take a broader view, we might ask why the discussion *should* focus on Phillip's book. Clearly, Susan's narrative, raising the issue of animal cruelty, could affect them in a way that Newsman Ned's adventures might not. Why should the book take priority over her story if hers is more discussable? Could the seemingly digressive story swapping be a good way to learn—about mousetraps and each other?

Any examination of talk in schools confronts a massive paradox. On the one hand, talk is the medium of instruction; it is one major way we accomplish objectives, measure learning. On the other, it eludes control, slips into unexpected territory. Talk generates more talk. Stories beget stories, and, before you know it, you're discussing mousetraps. It's like catching a butterfly—the more firmly you hold it, the more likely you are to kill it. And why catch it at all?

The research on classroom talk suggests that teachers normally keep the butterfly tightly between their fingers. A number of studies have shown we outtalk the entire class by a ratio of three to one (Goodlad, 1984, 229; Wells, 1985, 86). We ask anywhere from eighty to three hundred questions per hour (Dillon, 1988; Weber and Shake, 1988)—that's a question every twelve seconds! Teachers ask four to six times as many questions as the entire class (Mehan, 1979), and most student questions are procedural ("Does it have to be in ink?"). John Goodlad, author of *A Place Called School* (1984), concludes that "if teachers in the talking mode and students in the listening mode is what we want, rest assured that we have it" (229).

Teacher talk dominates most classrooms because discussions tend to fall into an initiate-respond-evaluate pattern (Mehan, 1979). The teacher asks a question, and students bid for the right to answer it by raising hands; the selected student responds by answering the question; and the teacher then makes some evaluative comment about the answer. ("Yes." "Uh-huh." "Very good.") Then the cycle begins again—with the teacher always taking two out of the three turns. Courtney Cazden (1988) has called the initiate-respond-evaluate sequence the default position of classroom discussion, the pattern we (and students) effortlessly fall into.

Pat McLure's classroom doesn't fit this pattern. Before beginning this book, I had spent considerable time there, and I was consistently impressed by the ways in which children seemed to control the talk (although Pat was by no means inactive). I was struck by her silences and by her capacity to listen. I wanted to know more about this talk, these silences. We decided to focus on the thirty- to forty-five-minute book discussions that occurred each day at 9:30. Our methodology (if it can be called that) was brutally simple. Each week, I would sit in on a group and tape-record it, also making written notes so that I could distinguish speakers when I transcribed. In the intervals between visits, I would transcribe the discussion, using only the left-hand half of each page. Sometimes I would insert questions; for example, I might ask Pat why she thought a student wasn't participating. She would then read through the transcript, annotating it in the blank right-hand half of the page. She would answer my questions, make observations about the response styles of students, describe decisions she made, or show how the discussion fit into other parts of the school day. If effect, she helped me see the discussion through her eyes. By the end of the year, we had almost eight hundred pages of transcripts with about twelve hundred annotations.

With transcripts in hand, we next moved into the "so what?" stage. We had interesting data, lively transcripts, but no interpretive frame, no governing metaphor, for looking at them. Our early presentations were like vacation slide shows: "Here's a . . . " "Now here we have . . . " I remember after one presentation a teacher asked, "What have you learned from this?" This was not a trick question, but I had trouble answering it. I felt, sheepishly, like one of my composition students caught without a point. "So what?"

My efforts to impose order took me through a number of false starts that, in retrospect, are instructive. One of them was to begin by culling those examples of talk that showed students at their analytic best, moments of precociousness, exchanges that we would be delighted to hear from mature readers. The tendency to highlight the superlative—and, by omission, to suggest that the ordinary does not exist—is more common in writing/reading-process literature than any of us would like to admit. Special moments seem to be convincing evidence of success. They sell the approach, but they misrepresent it as well. The ordinary, nonprecocious moments are more common, and, in the end, they are surely more significant.

Another false start was to see modeling as the key. I was well aware of Bruner's work on scaffolding (1985) and of ways in which this metaphor has been used to describe writing conferences

(Sowers, 1985). The teacher demonstrates a skill and provides structured help, gradually transferring responsibility until the external
prompts are no longer needed. Pearson and Gallagher write:

> Any academic task can be conceptualized as requiring different
> proportions of teacher and student responsibility. . . . When the
> teacher is taking all or most of the responsibility for the task
> completion, he is "modeling" or demonstrating the desired
> application of some strategy. When the student is taking all or
> most of the responsibility, she is "practicing" or "applying" that
> strategy. What comes in between these two extremes is the
> gradual release of responsibility from teacher to students or . . .
> "guided practice." (1983, 337–38)

Some of what I saw in the transcripts seemed to fit this model
of transferring responsibility. For example, Pat initially modeled the
follow-up questions that pushed students to offer reasons for
choices, and, very quickly, students began asking the "why" questions, just as the release-of-responsibility model suggests. But despite
the elegance of this interpretation, the more I looked at the transcripts, the more inadequate the model seemed.

In the first place, the theory behind modeling often implies that
what counts is that which the teacher models and students pick up.
Children are seen as bereft of significant strategies (ones that count)
when they begin a task. Growth is defined as the progressive inter-
nalization of adult models. It is easy, then, to dismiss as insignificant
or deviant or irrelevant talk that does not match the modeled behavior of the teacher.

What we have is the one-way socialization of children into the
adult mode of discussion. According to Hugh Mehan (1980), the
prevailing models of socialization "only focus on the influence of
society on the uninitiated member of society. They do not give equal
consideration to the contribution of the uninitiated member in the
socialization process" (147). This unidirectional focus tends to por-
tray socialization as "the pouring of cultural knowledge from vessels
that are full of cultural knowledge (e.g. adults) to empty vessels
(children)" (147).

Suppose we take the example of coaching a first- and second-
grade soccer team, a task I took on during my recent sabbatical. To

a degree, my job was to initiate the players into some characteristics of the adult game. I taught them rules they didn't know and strategies they tended not to use (e.g., passing—they all wanted to dribble and score). But to be effective, I had to be initiated into the game as they invented it. The first thing I did (partly out of desperation) was to watch them play a scrimmage game. Instead of assuming all the responsibility, I assumed almost none. And the game they invented made sense. The top player on each side would take the ball down the center toward the goal and try to shoot. My instinct was to yell "Pass," but, as I watched, I saw the reasoning behind the strategy: If the top player passed off, he or she probably wouldn't get the ball again.

I began to see my role as grafting parts of the adult game onto the game that they had invented. I tried, for example, to make them more mindful of being in position instead of *always* chasing the ball. But to induct them into the game as I envisioned it, I needed to understand and respect the game as they played it. My least success-ful moments occurred when I took full responsibility for demonstrat-ing a strategy; I lost them almost every time.

In addition to being adult centered, all of my false starts at analyzing the transcripts failed to account for many of the most lively moments in discussions. Take, for example, the exchanges that occurred after Susan had shared *Thomas the Rabbit* (Lloyd, 1984) and the children were talking about Thomas getting out of a trap. When Adam said that it was too bad that Thomas got away, Susan shot back, "Do you want him to become rabbit stew?" Her comment initiated a discussion of semigross foods.

Martin: Have you ever had rabbit stew?

Susan: Uh-uh. My mother has had pickled rabbit.

Adam: It is good?

Susan: I never had it before. I don't even want to eat it.

Jed: My mom likes frog legs.

Adam: My mother loves them and she loves snails.

Susan: Has she been to Canada yet?

Adam: Yes.

Susan: No wonder.

Jed: Well, Thomas is sort of like Dumbo but he's a rabbit.

Susan: And he can't fly. He can sort of fly, he can go so fast.

Jed: Yeah. Ooup [*sound effect indicating speed*]. And then you couldn't say he has frog legs.

Phillip: It sort of grosses me out. If I hear it more than five times a day I get sick.

Martin: Frog legs, frog legs, frog legs, frog legs, frog legs.

Phillip: No, that's not what I'm talking about. The other way will do it.

Jed: I eat frog legs. I eat frog legs. I eat frog legs.

Adam: You eat frog legs. You eat frog legs. You eat frog legs. You eat frog legs. You eat frog legs.

Phillip: I eat frog legs [*pretends to throw up*].

Pat did not model this kind of exchange. She did not teach Jed the strategy of using sound effects to indicate speed. She did not construct an instructional scaffolding to teach this routine. At times like these, she is allowing the oral culture of her students into the classroom conversation. In the exchange above, we can see the fascination with what is "gross" (one of my six-year-old son's favorite words is "barf"). We see the ritual of calling Phillip's bluff and Phillip playing along with the game.

I should add that the culture that we see in this exchange is particularly male. Vivian Paley (1984) has noted that, at about this time, children "think they invented the differences between boys and girls and, as with any new invention, must prove that it works" (ix). When I first read this transcript, I found it funny, as did many of the people I shared it with. But a feminist friend came up to me after a presentation and said, "Did you notice in that transcript how Susan stops talking once the boys take over? When I was a kid in school that used to make me so mad!" She was right. Susan didn't play that game.

It was often at these moments—when students moved away from the modeled forms of responses—that the groups seemed most alive. Clearly, I needed a perspective that would enable me to take seriously the talk that did not fit preconceived adult models, just as I had come to respect the soccer game that the children had invented. I began to look at the reading discussions as examples of the meeting and interaction of two cultures, the adult culture represented by the teacher and her questions and the culture of six-, seven-, and eight-year-olds, with both contributing to the success of the group. The child culture brings in habits of responding to texts that are not adultlike (e.g., sound effects, reenactments, wordplay). The range of response is therefore richer. This culture also contributes conviviality, camaraderie, and humor. The adult questions and comments expand the repertoire with which students are already equipped, pushing them to think in more elaborated ways— for example, stating reasons for opinions.

The term *culture* is normally used to indicate racial, ethnic, socioeconomic, or regional characteristics. By that definition, these children would be considered part of Pat's culture (white, middle class, semirural). By using it to examine children's talk, we are challenged to grant that talk an integrity that we might otherwise withhold. If children seem to go consistently "off task," we can ask if both cultures share the same definition of *task*. If children seem to change the subject, we can ask whether their notion of subject is the same as ours. We are challenged to take children's humor seriously and to look at the role it plays in the reading groups. We don't turn differences into deficits. Finally, we are challenged to believe that children come to these groups not as total novices but as members of a rich oral culture that has its own repertoire of responses.

Let me add that this is not a brilliant discovery. Over twenty years ago, Basil Bernstein wrote:

> If the culture of the teacher is to be part of the consciousness of the child, then the culture of the child must first be in the consciousness of the teacher. . . . We should start knowing that the social experience the child already possesses is valid and significant, and that this social experience should be reflected back to him as being valid and significant. (1966, 120)

More recently (indeed after this book was substantially written), I found novelist Alison Lurie making the same point in her book *Don't Tell the Grown-Ups.*

> [T]o an adult much of the folklore of childhood may sound trivial or even meaningless. This is to make the same kind of mistake that early explorers made when they couldn't understand the stories and jokes told in other cultures. Later on,

anthropologists who took the time to study these societies understood their folklore—indeed, studying the folklore was one of the ways they came to understand the society.

Anyone who has spent time around children and observed them carefully, or really remembers what it was to be a child, knows that childhood is a separate culture, with its own, largely oral, literature. Childhood, in this sense, is a primitive society— or rather, several primitive societies leading into the other. (1990, 194)

I also felt that, by viewing talk as a meeting of cultures, I could better account for the motivation of students. If the only talk that matters is that which is patterned off adult conversation, students can conclude that what matters most to them, their culture, has little place in the classroom. That was certainly my experience in elementary school. I felt my interest in sports, in any contest of strength or speed or physical skill, was irrelevant to school.

Then, in third grade, I had Mrs. Fulton, a mother of grown boys, impossibly old by our standards, at least forty. She was uncertified, years short of a bachelor's degree, and her lack of preparation worried some of the parents. But she knew something about boys and what mattered to them. At recess, she didn't stand around or do a token turn of the girls' jumprope. This ancient woman joined us for football. As I recall, she was left-handed, and her passes, though they had a higher arc than ours, were just as good. I don't think any of us had ever seen a grown woman throw a football, let alone throw it well (this was, after all, the late fifties, when adults didn't even walk). That gesture on the playground helped ensure our cooperation in the classroom. She had recognized, even participated in, our culture. And we would participate in hers.

To introduce these two cultures at work, I will describe an entire day in Pat's class. It is March 20, 1990, the last day of winter, the day the "Russian Lady" comes to visit.

2

March 20, 1990

7:50 A.M. THE LAST SPRING thaw has melted all but the largest snow piles. We're into frost-heave season now. An indecisive February and early March have turned most of the local roads into a series of natural speed bumps that expose the poor suspension in my Toyota. Mast Road is no exception. It runs the length of Lee, New Hampshire, one of those New England towns that barely have a center—a police station, church, convenience store, and then you're past it. The road gets its name from the mast-building industry that flourished in Lee and Barrington in the early 1700s. Tall white cedar was cut and transported along the Mast Way to Durham Point and the floated down the Piscataqua River to Portsmouth, which was then (and to some degree is still) known for shipbuilding.

If the road has strong regional associations, Mast Way School could be anywhere. A one-story, brick T of a building, it resembles schools built all over the country to handle the post–World War II babyboomers. The floors are the same nine-inch linoleum squares that I used to stare at during endless oral reports about the continents.

8:05 A.M. Pat McLure's combined first/second-grade class (fourteen first graders, nine second graders) is located at one end of the T. She has been teaching at the school for seventeen years—she's a veteran. When people ask why she stays there (a number of her colleagues have gone to the newly opened elementary school), she gestures half-seriously to the accumulation of "stuff" on the walls, in the work areas. "I just can't move it all."

I once counted twenty-five lists on her walls—of numbers, color names, the alphabet, logo directions, bus routes, contractions, names of the days of the week. (Figure 2–1 is a student rendering.) She has posted three calendars (including one incubating calendar), book posters, and two quilts. One of the quilts was made by the class three years before, each child contributing a square. Pat points out the square contributed by Brenda Miller, a researcher in her class that year, on which was drawn, with an indelible marker, two chicks—each with four legs.

Late March is chick time in Pat's room. Since she began teaching at Mast Way, she has arranged, each spring, to bring in an incubator and fertilized eggs. Children learn to candle the eggs to see if they

13

Figure 2–1   Pat McLure's classroom as drawn by one of her students

truly are fertilized, and they turn the eggs daily to ensure even distribution of heat. Chicks become the focus of their science learning, their vocabulary learning, their drawing, and their writing.

This year, Pat has added brood hens to the project, two Silkies, brought into the class yesterday. Silkies, as the name implies, have fine, fluffy feathers, and they are known for their calm dispositions. "Calm" seems to be an understatement; they appear catatonic. They don't move, barely breathe, make no noise, and seem indifferent to each other. They just sit.

She rents the brood hens (and an incubator) from a Barrington resident, Sylvia Townsend, who has developed a school project that she calls "Sylvia's Something to Crow About." It comes with a five-page list of advice and folk wisdom (e.g., "DO NOT LET THE TEMPERATURE GO OVER 101 DEGREES—this will cook the eggs in a very short time"). She reminds kids that chicks "come out all wet and gooey, and they have to mess, plop, do their duty, any way you call it." At the end of the five pages, Sylvia undercuts her authority in typical New Hampshire style: "No, I don't 'know it all,' but I've made most of the mistakes."

8:35 A.M.   The bell rings. The children come into the school, hanging their coats on hooks in the hallway. The first stop in the classroom is the chicken pen. "They're staring at me," says Abby.

"Well, stare back at them," says Corrine.

The day begins without formalities—no morning announcements, no pledge to the flag, no reminders about what the children need to do. First, they turn over their name card. Each child has a four-by-six-inch laminated card with his or her photograph at the top. At the beginning of the day, all the cards are tucked into a line of pockets so that the photos are not visible. After they are turned over, Pat can take attendance at a glance. Then the children take their blue writing folders out of a plastic crate and begin to write.

Class friendships find their way into stories. Jake and Adam are collaborating on a ghost story in which they are the main characters. Jake is also featured in Sandy's story, in which they both throw dynamite at Count Dracula. Michelle is writing an information book about herself and her friend Jennifer, while Jennifer starts on a story about a cat and a mouse and a bird. Corrine, who was in Pat's class last year, writes a "guess book," in which she provides clues to someone in the class.

Billy continues to work on the story that has occupied him for the past three weeks, "Cloudy with a Chance of Lettuce," a take-off on *Cloudy with a Chance of Meatballs* (Barrett, 1978). He admires the last page that he drew, which features an "egg atak," with eggs parachuting down from a command ship (thus introducing the theme of war, so popular with the boys). Instead of continuing the story today, he draws a jet plane—one of his specialities. Pat admits to wondering how long she should allow Billy to continue with the same story.

Pat makes the rounds of children, beginning with Allan, who has drawn a Philly Billy that looks to me like one of the wizards in Martin Handford's *Waldo* books, which have captivated Allan and his friend Rob. Later in the day, Rob will work on his own "Find the Wizard" drawing.

While his classmates begin to write, Scott picks up the "job can" to start on the central organizing task of the day. An empty coffee can covered with worn contact paper, the job can isn't much to look at.

Glued to it are several small laundry hooks with job labels above them—"reading share group," "snack," "lunch," "pencils." Scott's job is to recruit classmates for these jobs. He studies the attendance board and then sets before him the small wooden name tags of every student in attendance. For each job, he checks the rolled-up list kept inside the can that indicates the names of those who have done the job recently and the dates they did it. He offers each job to someone who has not performed it recently, and, once the person has agreed, Scott writes the name and date on the list and places the name tag on the hook below the job. Billy, who by this time has lost interest in "Cloudy with a Chance of Lettuce," lobbies for, and gets, the lunch job.

8:55 A.M. Scott has finished his work on the job can. Jimmy, a second-grade veteran, has been given the job of "sign up," probably the second most critical job in the classroom. Like Scott, Jimmy must consult a list, this one indicating those who have recently shared their reading and writing with the entire class. Thus informed, he walks around the room with a clipboard, asking people to share their writing. Melanie, Scott, and Corrine agree to share, and Jimmy takes for himself the last slot. He places the clipboard on the chalk ledge in the community area in the corner of the room. It is 9:00, and the responsibilities for the entire day are already set—without any guidance or coaxing from Pat. Earlier in the year, it wasn't so automatic (see Figure 2–2).

At this point, Scott has returned to his own story, a space adventure that he and his friend Jed are in. He draws a picture of their ship landing on an ice field. He then turns to Jed and breaks the bad news.

"See. We landed in a bad place, Jed."

Jed looks at the picture. "There's an airplane. We'll fill our gas tanks from it."

Scott, shaking his head, says, "We're in outer space. I hope you know."

"We'll use a gun to attack it."

"These ships are gunproof."

"We invent a bomb."

Scott, a little impatient with Jed, explains, "We're going to climb into their ship and take it over."

At Scott's table, Tommy is writing a *Mario 2* story modeled after a Nintendo game in which a princess is saved. Jed, after kibitzing with

Figure 2–2   Students new to the "job can" feature of Pat's classroom can become a bit frustrated

Scott, begins his own space adventure story and asks Scott if he wants to be in it.

9:15 A.M.   Time for writing share group in the community area. Melanie, a first grader, sits in the Author's Chair, a small, antique visiting rocker. She reads the first two sentences that she has written for her story "Chicks and Ducks"—"I like chicks and ducks. They are warm and fuzzy." She then adds the ritual invocation to discussion, "Any comments or questions?"

Abby raises her hand, and Melanie calls on her. "I'm writing a book about a chick and I went to my friend Max's house and when we watched the baby goats eat they reminded me of chicks—the way they eat in a cluster."

Melanie doesn't respond. Phillip raises his hand and says that he likes her picture of the bird.

Melanie responds, "It's not a bird, it's a chick."

Jake says, "Chicks are birds."

17

For the first time, Pat, who has been taking notes on the discussion, enters it. "Is it going to be true?" This planning question puzzles Melanie, who doesn't answer it directly.

Sandy asks, "Do you know what you're going to write next?"

"Yeah."

"What?"

Melanie shrugs.

Pat concludes this sharing with an invitation to read more of the story later.

Like the center of Lee, Melanie's turn flashes by in a few seconds. Blink, and you've missed it. But that afternoon, Pat would see Melanie's willingness to share as one of the day's key events. Hindered by a lack of kindergarten, a November move to Lee, and frequent winter absences, Melanie is finally beginning to fit in.

Scott, whose morning has been very busy with his "job can" duties, reads his space adventure. Megan asks, "Do you know who was in the spaceship?"

"If you want to be in you can be and Jed wants to be in."

These stories, outlandish (literally) as they seem, serve a very practical purpose of defining friendship networks. Seconds later, Billy asks who's on the ship.

"Jed's on it, Allan, and Megan but a different Megan. Not Megan Evans [the Megan in the class]."

Jennifer asks, "What's Megan's last name?"

"Harder."

Allan asks, "Do you know any Megan Harder?"

"No, but I know a Laura Harder."

This is a new way of fictionalizing for the class. Pat explains later that, because of some hurt feelings earlier in the year, classmates have to give permission for their names to be used in stories. Megan Evans had not yet given permission, so Scott worked around that constraint by inventing a fictional name from two real ones.

9:25 A.M. The morning meeting is over. Students take their red reading folders from another plastic crate and head for the desks. Corrine, who has been assigned the job of setting up the reading share group, asks class members if they are ready to share. To be ready, they have to have completed a process outlined on the photocopied reading log in their folders: they need to pick a book and practice reading it alone; they need to read the book to a partner and talk about it with that person; they need to complete a book page by drawing a picture from the book and writing a comment at the bottom of the page. By the time students meet to share their books, they are familiar with them.

9:30 A.M.   Corrine has picked Cindy, Martin, and Scott to be in her group. They sit around a circular table in the exact center of the room. Corrine, as leader, determines the order of the sharing and places herself last of the four. Each student takes a turn lasting from five to fifteen minutes depending on the discussion. And each turn takes a predictable, almost ritualistic form: the student names the book's title and author (which Pat notes in her record of the book sharing conferences), provides a summary or general sense of the book, reads a part of the book, and, once finished, asks for comments and questions, calling on members of the group who raise their hands. Early in the year, children had difficulty with this procedure; they would want to begin by reading and would have trouble planning which part of the book to read, preferring to read the whole thing. By now, the procedures are comfortably in place.

Cindy begins with James Stevenson's *Could Be Worse* (1977). "It's about this grandfather, and he always says the same thing every day. And he eats the same thing and he reads the same thing, and one day he makes something up because the grandchildren think that the grandfather is boring." Cindy has deftly set up her story, summarizing up to the point where she is going to begin reading.

She reads about the grandfather's adventures, drawing a giggle from Corrine when she comes to the marmalade attack. When Cindy gets to the last page, where Grandfather asks the children in the story what they thought of his adventure, Scott and Corrine join her for the children's reply, "Could be worse." They know this book.

At this point in the year, the class has developed a number of frequently asked questions, and Corrine begins with one of them, "Would you like that to happen to you?"

Cindy (joined by Scott) almost shouts the response, "No way."

Martin follows with the most frequently asked question, "What's your favorite page?" Cindy shows the picture of the giant snowball coming at Grandpa. Martin follows with the automatic follow-up question, "Why is that your favorite page?"

"Because it looks pretty funny."

Pat, who has been taking notes on the discussion, comes in for the first time a couple of exchanges later, after Corrine says that her favorite page was the marmalade attack. "I was interested in that marmalade, too. Where does Grandpa find all of those things to put into the story?"

Scott takes a try. "Maybe he had a dream and he wrote down what he dreamed."

Cindy follows. "Maybe. But he also wanted the kids to think he's not boring." And, as she talks, she moves toward an insight. "So maybe he just thought of that because he ate marmalade and he ate toast."

Pat supports this answer. "That's right, toast was in it, too. And his newspaper was in it, too."

"He probably had goldfish then."

Martin adds, "He could have had a big huge lobster."

Cindy's turn ends with the group connecting elements of the story in this way.

The discussions of *Could Be Worse* and the next book, *George and Martha Back in Town* (Marshall, 1984), proceed effortlessly, almost casually. The books are familiar, and the children read them with expression. Scott's choice, *St. George and the Dragon* (Hodges, 1984), follows a different pattern. Although Pat had read this book to the class the previous week, it was not familiar to the group, and the difficult, almost archaic language (e.g., "bade") poses a real challenge to Scott, who had been reading *Clifford* books only a couple of months earlier. The standard reading textbooks would say that Scott is reading at the "frustrational level"—but nobody has bothered to tell Scott, who is anything but frustrated.

He plows ahead, stopping in almost every sentence for assistance ("huge," "reared," "monstrous," "horrible," "round," "hundred," "stings," "burning," "speckled," "breast," "withstand," "barbed"). On the third page of the book, Scott begins to skip lines, and I lose the thread of the story. Cindy and Corrine seem to lose interest. Only Pat and Scott's loyal friend Martin seem with him. For the first time in the session, I'm uncomfortable and wonder why Pat lets Scott go on so long—eight minutes, the longest reading segment of the session. It is clear to me that Scott has picked too hard a book and should probably be coaxed back toward books like the ones the others had chosen.

Later I talked to Pat and realized that I was taking my cue from how *I* felt about the reading. I was uncomfortable, but Scott wasn't—he wanted to go on to a fourth page. Pat reminded me of how Scott had read the *Clifford* books in November, through rough approximations and reconstructions based on the picture cues. He had developed a style of pushing his reading forward—picking difficult books and handling them as best he could—in which his tolerance for imprecision was an asset.

10:00 A.M.   Snacktime. Lunchboxes appear, bearing the insignia of perennial favorites like Mickey Mouse and Looney Toons, durable ones like G.I. Joe, and those whose time has passed (My Little Pony). The food is even more various than the lunchboxes—string cheese, cookies, peanut butter crackers, and fruit rollups with punch-out characters. Pat sips a midmorning coffee at the reading table, where she is joined by Abby, who tells her about a funny chapter in Patricia Reilly Giff's *In the Dinosaur's Paw* (1985).

Near the end of snacktime, John Lowy, the principal, announces over the loudspeaker that it has begun to rain and recess will be indoors. Again, without a word from Pat, the children walk over to the attendance board, where each picks an area marker out of an old cocoa tin and places it in front of his or her attendance card. Children then move to the areas—science, writing, art, math, computers—indicated on the markers they've chosen. Scott, Martin, and Billy draw jets. Rob works on his *Waldo* book. Sandy, Jake, and Jed play with a set of magnets, and Jed, the youngest of the group, comes to Pat twice during the period to complain of unfairness.

Tommy and Phillip play with the LOGO program on the Apple computer in the corner of the room. They try to make the LOGO turtle take such long steps that the screen will be filled with lines, completely green. They type *FD1234,* and a line races to the top of the screen and then reenters at the bottom again and again, until the screen is a network of lines. Tommy types (I think by accident) *FRT1234,* and the user-friendly program responds, "I DO NOT KNOW HOW TO FRT."

"Look," Tommy says, "it doesn't know how to fart."

10:48 A.M.   Scott has replaced the area markers in the cocoa tin, and the reading group has reassembled to ask Scott questions. If his book was somewhat unusual, the questions are not. They are the old standards: What's your favorite page? Why is that your favorite page? Who's your favorite character? Have you read any other books by this author? Why did you choose that book? Because Scott has heard these questions (and asked them himself) so many times, he is comfortable with them, ready to answer.

When Scott mentions that he likes books about dragons, Pat, in her librarian role, mentions *The Popcorn Dragon* (Thayer, 1989). Does Scott know it? No, but he's read a book about a "little boy who makes a dragon become good." Pat is reminded of *The Little Knight* (Johnson, 1957), about a boy who is the friend of a dragon who is unhappy because no one likes him. This listing of possible books for future reading is a common feature at the end of each turn.

The next book, *Imogene's Antlers* (Small, 1985), is more familiar to the group, and they all anticipate their favorite parts—the mother's fainting and the ending, when Imogene, to her family's relief, loses her antlers, only to reveal a magnificent peacock tail.

Scott asks, "What if that was a chapter book? Now she would have all that trouble with peacock feathers. Then she'd . . . "

Corrine picks up the idea. "Then she'd have . . . horse feet."

"That's what would come after that?" Pat asks. "She'd wake up on Saturday morning with horse feet?"

"Yeah, and she'd have hoofs instead of feet. And she'd have to walk around like a horse. And her mother would faint. And she would be making lots of noise."

Martin and Scott together: "Thud, thud, thud, thud. Thud, thud, thud, thud."

11:02 A.M. Math. For the first—and only—time in the day, first and second graders are separated. The thirteen first graders gather in a semicircle in the community area, while the second graders work independently. Pat dumps out hundreds of popsicle sticks. For a while, the children marvel at the sheer number of them, perhaps thinking back to the popsicles in which they were once embedded. "How many do we have here?" she asks.

Billy answers instantly, "1,006."

Pat asks the children to pull sticks from the pile and group them in bundles of ten. Most students are able to make four or five bundles before Pat calls time. She asks students to tell her how many bundles they have made and how many sticks are in their bundles altogether. When it's Scott's turn, he says, "I have fourteen bundles and I don't know how many sticks." Pat leads the class in counting by tens to 140. After some more practice, the children each use the tens bundles and single sticks to indicate the units in specific numbers. As turns move around the group, several boys are clearly getting bored. Jed says to his friends, "I'm sort of tired." Phillip agrees. Billy, the most restless boy in the class, says he can hardly wait until lunch.

After about twenty minutes with the sticks, Pat dismisses the group so that they can work on math papers posing problems similar to those they had figured out with the sticks. As Billy goes to a desk, he says to Pat, "I still think there's 1,006."

11:40 A.M.   After math, the entire class reassembles for the second whole class sharing session that Jimmy had scheduled three hours before. Corrine takes the Author's Chair and reads Trinka Hakes Noble's *The Day Jimmy's Boa Ate the Wash* (1980), the story of a catastrophic field trip to a farm. The class goes "Oooh" when pigs in the story eat the children's lunch—serious business at this time of day.

Abby says, "And the teacher doesn't even care."

Pat, in mock defense of teachers, answers, "I would care."

As Corrine holds the book up to show one of the pictures, the pages fall out, leaving Corrine with just the cover. Abby jokes, "Jimmy's boa eats the book."

If there is a common quality in most of the books shared today—*Could Be Worse, George and Martha Back in Town, Imogene's Antlers,* and *The Day Jimmy's Boa Ate the Wash*—it is humor. I wonder, as I listen, whether we fully appreciate the central role of humor in children's literature. Nothing seems to draw the members of this class together so much as laughing at books. Do children laugh when they read basal readers? I wonder.

11:52 A.M.   The class stays in the community area after Corrine has finished with her book. Pat turns to a different notebook and asks if anyone has a word for the day to spell. Phillip begins with *voit.*

Pat asks, "Voit?"

"Yeah. Voit. It's on my tennis shoe. V-O-I-T." And so begins a list of spelling words that will never be found on any published list.

Michelle spells *Susan*—classmates' names are popular. Cindy picks *Abiyoyo,* the title of one of her favorite reading books. Jake picks *Beaver County,* a place in Pennsylvania that he had visited with his family (he's wearing a Beaver County hat—but he doesn't look). When Melanie, after two tries, spells *Mrs. McLure* correctly she gets a cheer from the class. Jennifer picks *lottery*—she explains that her mother has just won $1,000 in the lottery. And so on.

Sometimes Pat uses this time to teach a skills lesson. On a newsprint page taped to the wall, for example, is a list of contractions that the class has generated when someone in the class picked a contraction for her word. On another day, Pat might ask the class to make a list of words with the same structure (e.g., those ending in *ght*).

After each child has spelled a word, Allan hands out the spelling books, thirteen dittoed pages, front and back, with a page for each letter and with the traditional bold lines to mark the height of capital letters and broken lines to indicate the height of many of the small letters. The students write their words for the day and bring their books to Pat for her to check them off. This is the only time in the day when Pat, in her words, "gets fussy" about handwriting, encouraging Martin, for example, to make the *h* of his word *hen* taller.

After Pat collects the books, children reassemble in the community area to be dismissed for lunch. By this point, the rhythm of the day is clear to me—there is a steady flow from communal activity to individual and small-group work, from the more structured (but certainly not restrictive) talk and turn taking that occur when the whole class meets to the casual talk at the desks, from the compact feeling of the community area to the feeling of dispersal when children work in various areas of the classroom. Back and forth.

12:07 P.M. Billy finally gets to do the job he lobbied for at the beginning of the day. He sits in the rocking chair, smiling his wonderfully crooked smile, and calls children to get into the lunch line. As each child's name is called, he or she passes by Pat, who hands out a lunch ticket.

12:15 P.M.–1:05 P.M. Lunch and play outside (the rain has stopped). I join Michelle, Martin, Corrine, and Scott for lunch. If education has changed since I went to school, school lunches haven't. Today's fare is a very dry hamburger that sticks to the bread and limp french fries still covered with cooking oil. Scott hides Martin's gloves and repeats in his best criminal voice, "I love stealing people's gloves. I love stealing people's gloves." The monitor rings a bell, signaling for quiet, and dismisses the tables one by one. Children gather the balls and jump ropes that they had placed on the stage earlier and head out into the mud.

1:05 P.M.   Children come in from the playground and hang up their coats on the hooks outside the class—a quicker process now that they're not wearing the one-piece snowsuits that make them look like miniature astronauts. Sandy, who always moves at her own pace, is the last of the class to move into the community area where Pat already sits in the Author's Chair, ready to read Stephen Kellogg's *Chicken Little* (1985). Only later do I realize how this book choice fits into the chicken phase that the class is entering.

Finally, as Sandy settles into the group, Pat reads the title, and someone asks who started the story. Rob answers, "The real version was so long ago that no one knew who made it up." Pat (as librarian) asks who has read any of the other Stephen Kellogg folktales, and children mention *Paul Bunyan* (1988) and *Johnny Appleseed* (1988). By now, this pattern of suggestion is familiar—each book shared leads to a suggestion for several more to read. When people ask how children are able to choose their own books, they need to realize the number of possibilities that are set before children. My guess is that the real problem for them is not finding a book but finding only one.

Pat asks about the word *poultry* (in one of the pictures in the book, a poultry truck is repainted as a police truck). Melanie answers, "Birds." This is the second time today that she has played with the category *birds*—recall that earlier she claimed that chicks weren't birds. Pat says that poultry are birds that we eat for food, and the class quickly makes a small list: turkey, duck, chicken, goose.

Before she reads, Pat also notes the dedication at the front of the book. Pat regularly has students attend to the conventions of books that fall outside the stories themselves—the copyright page, the list of the author's works, information about the author and illustrator, the table of contents, and, today, the dedication page. It's possible that this brief reference will spawn dedication pages in their own writing.

As Pat reads the story, the class is totally attentive, as focused as they've been all day. They laugh when a helicopter with the word *Sky* written on it falls on the police van driven by the wolf (the sky does fall in this version). When she finishes, Scott says that the book reminds him of the "Chicken Little" play he was in in kindergarten. Pat asks if it was the same version.

"A little different. They reached the king or the wolf disguised as the king."

Pat observes, "They didn't get to the king in this version."

1:19 P.M.   Silent reading for ten minutes. Children quickly choose books and take their seats. Pat reads an article by Gordon Wells that a colleague has given her. This is the first time all day that the room has been completely still, and it seems almost empty, a kind of void. I'm sure the normal noise level of this class would bother some teachers. Talk is so often considered the enemy of work. But in this class, talk is the sea upon which everything else floats. Peaceful as these ten minutes are, I'm almost relieved when conversation returns.

1:31 P.M.   The class reassembles in the community area, Sandy again the last one to arrive, singing the last lines of Pete Seeger's *Abiyoyo* (1985). Pat explains that it is now free choice time, a time to finish up other work. As they did prior to the indoor recess in the morning, children pick areas and put the area markers in front of their cards on the attendance board.

1:39 P.M.   Cindy finishes work on a paper bag puppet, which she shows to Jake and Allan, who are sitting at her table.

"I'm Mr. Big Eye."

"Mr. Big Guy?"

"Mr. Big *Eye.*"

"How can a girl be Mr. Big Guy?"

1:45 P.M.   Megan and Joyce hide behind the pen for the brood hens and work on paper bag butterfly heads to which they will attach

wings. They seem to take as their model the butterfly in Eric Carle's
A Very Hungry Caterpillar (1981).

1:47 P.M.   Allan works on his *Where's Wizard?* book, a take-off on
Where's Waldo? (Handford, 1987), while his friend Rob is working
on coded messages that will provide clues for his own *Waldo*-
inspired book.

1:55 P.M.   The Soviet visitor arrives. We all knew she was coming,
but her entrance was more emphatic than Pat had anticipated. A very
erect middle-aged woman walks to the center of the classroom and
announces, "My name is Ksana Volodina and I am a teacher in the
Soviet Union and I would like to speak with you individually."

Jed asks Pat, "Is that the person who came from Italy?"

Ms. Volodina takes a seat at one of the desks and pulls out a
bag filled with star-shaped badges that she begins handing out
to the children who surround her. So much for speaking to them
individually.

"This is the badge of the baby Lenin. When children in the
Soviet Union turn six, they become Octobrists, and they begin wearing this badge." The picture of baby Lenin, molded into the center of
the star, looks for all the world like the Gerber baby—a warm engag-
ing smile, blond curly hair.

"Next I would like to give you some candy that our children
like. It is very hard and it is called 'Pulla' because it helps pull your
teeth out."

Phillip says loudly, "Good, I have a loose tooth."

A little tentatively—perhaps thinking of years of candy-from-
strangers warnings—they begin to chew on the candy. After a couple
of minutes, Corrine informs Pat that Rob's teeth are stuck together.
Deadpan, Pat responds, "I guess we won't be hearing from him for
a while."

2:07 P.M.   As abruptly as she entered, Ms. Volodina gets up to leave,
thanking the children for being such good hosts. They return to their
work areas with the curly-haired baby Lenin pinned to their shirts.

2:13 P.M.   Jed and Billy complete an elaborate ramp in the block
area, using pieces of wood with holes bored in them just large

enough for a marble to pass through. If all goes according to Jed and Billy's plan, the marble will start its descent from a tall block platform, pass over a large wooden cylinder, and then roll down a steep slope to the floor. They start a marble down to test the plan, and it fails to negotiate the cylinder, spilling onto the floor.

2:15 P.M.   Jennifer finds the *Big Book,* an alphabet book on chicks that her sister helped write two years before when she was in Pat's class. Michelle, looking over her shoulder, asks for a turn, and Jennifer says she has to wait.

2:17 P.M.   Corrine's teeth stick together.

2:20 P.M.   Jake, whose father helped organize Ms. Volodina's visit, brings a blank book around for each person in the class to draw a picture in. He will give the finished book to her that evening.

2:23 P.M.   Phillip tries to finish up the math pages that he started this morning. The work, in his words, is "not cinchy." He still has trouble seeing the cluster of ten boxes on the work pages as equivalent to the number in the tens column. Pat later tells me that she is concerned because Phillip does not come to her (or to another classmate) when he has trouble.

2:25 P.M.   Joyce and Megan bring out their paper bag butterflies to show Pat. They move the bags so that the attached wings seem to flutter. Antennae project from the heads. The girls are working on an illustration project, picking a favorite illustrator and then working to duplicate an illustration using the same materials the artist used. A couple of weeks before, they shifted from Ezra Jack Keats to Eric Carle and, in the process, sparked an interest in Eric Carle among all the first graders.

2:27 P.M.   Allan asks Cindy if she can find the wizard in the book he has just finished.

2:32 P.M.   Phillip, finally done with his math pages, tells Pat that he saw the white hen wiggle when it sat down.

"That's the most anyone has seen them do." This is the first mention of the hens that I've heard since the beginning of the day.

2:35 P.M.   The class begins to assemble, one last time, in the community area. The free choice time seemed overlong to me. When I ask Pat about it, she agrees. She had thought the book discussion after lunch would go on longer. I'm relieved to see that I'm not the only one who has trouble predicting how long things will take.

Jimmy, who six hours earlier had signed himself up for this spot, takes the Author's Chair and holds his book to his chest. "I'm not going to tell anyone what it is."

Abby says, "I know what you're going to share. *Chickens Aren't the Only Ones*" (Heller, 1981).

Billy tries to sit among a group of girls, who push him away. "Stay away, pest."

Jed, referring to Rob's candy trouble, says philosophically, "Rob always believes what a person says about candy."

Finally, the class is assembled. They look tired as they sprawl on the rug. I wonder if those people calling for longer school days as the solution to the "educational crisis" have spent full days in schools.

Jimmy begins to read his book, an informational book on how chickens and other birds lay eggs and raise their young. In the questions and comments session, the class trades stories about experiences with birds and eggs. Sandy, always ready with a story, begins. "Once when I went to my friend's house, outside we found a bird's egg in two pieces. I was wondering what bird it was but we didn't have a dictionary so I couldn't find out."

Billy, who has something of a reputation for embellishing, follows. "I used to have a robin's nest right on my window. And once a chick fell out and I took two pictures, once when it fell out and once when it was grown."

Billy triggers Rob. "Once we had a bird's nest in the gutter. And when it rained we would have to clog the gutter."

This idea of protecting nests reminds Adam of an experience. "Once when I went for a walk I found a nest with eggs and my dad wouldn't let me take them in. I had to hold back my younger brother."

Adam's story reminds Jennifer of a time when she and her older sister found a pheasant's feather. Susan then tells of a time when her dog chased a mother pheasant and her baby.

When the stories are exhausted, Pat asks Jimmy to write the name of the book on a list of books about chickens that the class is compiling.

2:50 P.M.   Dismissal time. I look at the group and, with the possible exception of Billy, I don't see the suppressed energy seeking an outlet that I always associated with the end of a school day (I can still remember the time my elementary school ended—3:15). They seem ready, a bit tired but calm.

"I'm going to give you two clues at a time today."

"If you are wearing sneakers and your bus number has three tens and four ones, you can get ready."

"If you're wearing a bright-colored shirt and your bus number has eight tens and seven ones, you can get ready."

"If you're wearing a sweatshirt and your number has eight tens and zero ones, you can get ready."

After a few more pairs of clues, the community area is empty, and the children sit at their desks as the principal calls bus numbers over the loudspeaker. When their buses are called, they put their chairs on their desks and walk up the stem of the T toward the main office and the waiting buses.

3:05 P.M.   The day is over, the room empty except for Pat and me (and, of course, the unmoving, unresponsive brood hens). Pat mentions that it has been a calm day, even with the arrival of the Soviet visitor. This calmness, the seemingly effortless movement from activity to activity, disappoints some visitors to her class. Perhaps they expect the teacher to be a more dynamic center, someone who rouses students to action through sheer force of personality.

This image of teaching is deeply embedded in our culture. I remember recently seeing *Dead Poet's Society,* a movie that celebrates this kind of instruction. In one scene, Keating (played by Robin Williams) leads his timid, regimented students out of the classroom to contemplate the trophy case and reflect on the brevity of life. They follow him sheepishly (sheeplike). At the trophy case, he recites poetry ("Gather ye rosebuds while ye may . . . ") and preaches the philosophy of *carpe diem*. Clearly, Keating will be the savior of these poor souls. Yet, while dramatically effective, there is something of the Pied Piper in the scene as well. The students are dependent on Keating's dynamism and vision; they would be lost without him.

Pat's style is different, not less active but active in a different way. "I'm a resource. Setting the scene and then seeing what will happen and reacting to it is more my style—as opposed to making things happen with the kids first. This doesn't mean I don't take an active role in it. It's just different, a reacting role."

It's as if Pat creates the silences the students fill. I think back to Scott's eight-minute battle with *St. George and the Dragon*. In how many classes could he have gone on so long, uninterrupted?

3

I've Got Nine

WILLIAM JAMES, IN his *Talks to Teachers,* spoke of the absolutely essential role habit plays in our learning:

> The more the details of our daily life we can hand over to the effortless custodian of automatism, the more our higher powers of mind will be set free for their own proper work. There is no more miserable human being than one in whom nothing is habitual but indecision, and for whom the lighting of every cigar, the drinking of every cup, the time of rising and going to bed every day and the beginning of every bit of work are subjects of express volitional deliberation. Full half the time of the man goes to deciding or regretting of matters which ought to be so ingrained in him as practically not to exist for his consciousness at all. ([1900] 1958, 62)

The same can be said for the classroom. There is no classroom more unproductive than one in which there are no predictable routines. If neither students nor teachers know what kind of work is expected when, energy and time that might be spent on the work is expended instead on making decisions that should be habitual. When the open classrooms of the late sixties and early seventies failed, as they often did, it was because the movement's proponents tended to distrust all imposed order, trusting rather to the open, spontaneous decision making of teachers and students. For example, David Holbrook, a British educator, wrote in 1966:

> Good creative work can only be spontaneous and the teacher works best when he works with opportunities as they arise. Why children decide to take *hate* one week and *flowers* the next as themes is unpredictable, but it is necessary to important dynamics of their exploration of life to do so; and the creative teacher must follow, enlarge, and deepen. (Quoted in Dixon, 1967, 48)

Perhaps. But this spontaneity needs to be framed or bound by habitual work patterns. The accounts of creative writers also demonstrate the importance of regular (sometimes quasineurotic) work habits. According to Graham Greene, a writer must organize his or her life into "a mass of little habits" (quoted in Murray, 1990, 54). The same is true of classrooms.

35

There is little overt disciplining in Pat's class. Only rarely does she bring out "the evil eye," what some parents call "the look." During the entire year, I saw it only a handful of times, but it never failed to have an effect. To create "the look" she purses her lips (though not to the point of frowning), raises her eyebrows, and tilts her head slightly forward. It is not primarily an angry look. It is a serious look that expresses surprise and, to some degree, disappointment that someone has stepped out of line. When she brings out "the look," she usually lowers her voice, slows it down, the opposite of yelling. The effect is instantaneous. "I've worked for years to perfect that look," she says.

She rarely brings out the evil eye because of the rituals that are consistently observed in her classroom. Rituals might be viewed as socially shared habits that work to free members of a society from having to ponder every bit of behavior. We don't start from scratch in every situation. We seem to act naturally, spontaneously, but in fact we are guided by cultural norms and rituals. We are, to some degree, captives of these rituals (because we cease to think of them), but we are also freed by them to conduct, in William James's words, our "own proper work."

Once the reading share groups have been picked, they assemble in turn around the table at the center of the room, and the person who chose the group assigns the order, usually putting himself or herself last. Even when choices like this one (and choosing seats) are open, the class falls into a conventionalized pattern. Pat records the order on her Book Sharing Conference Sheet. Once the order is set, the first child on the list says the name of the book and the author, and again Pat writes these down. (Indeed, class members consider Pat's primary responsibility to be that of recorder.)

When students like Melanie have difficulty with this procedure, they often get help from more experienced members of the group. At the end of one turn, Melanie mentions that she can't get the song from *Abiyoyo* out of her mind.

Pat [jokingly]: Well, Melanie, if you can get over that—
Melanie [interrupting]: I can't.
Pat: —it's your turn.
Megan: What are you going to share?

Melanie: You'll see.
Megan: It's your turn.
Melanie: It's a book about . . .
Joyce [*gently*]: What's it called?
Melanie: It's called?
Joyce: Yeah, what's it called?
Melanie: The Farm Concert.
Joyce: Oh.
Melanie: It's about a farmer. . . .

In her comment on this exchange, Pat is uncharacteristically effusive. "I think this is great. They are cueing her in a helpful way. No one is putting Melanie down."

After Pat records the title and author, the book's presenter gives a summary or overview that Pat records close to verbatim in the comment section of her sheet. After the summary, the presenter reads a section from the book (or, in the case of shorter picture books, the entire book) and then asks, "Any comments or questions?" the ritualistic invitation for discussion to begin. This pattern is repeated for each turn, and it is identical to the pattern used in shares involving the whole class.

It often takes forty minutes to complete the four turns of a sharing group, a considerable amount of time for first graders, in particular, to sit around a table and listen. I am convinced that they are able to attend so well because of the predictable pattern of each turn. In this regard, I performed an inadvertent experiment at mid-year. I wanted to interview a group of first and second graders, so Pat arranged for me to take them to the music room. The students I picked usually had no trouble attending to the book shares for forty minutes, but about fifteen minutes into my interview I could see the first graders become restless. Billy even wandered over to try out a couple of instruments (I have it on tape). Aside from the unfortunate distractions of the music room, these first graders had trouble with the interview because it did not involve the same pattern of expectations they had for their sharing groups. It didn't have the predictable four-turn shape.

Within this familiar format, there are also formula questions that the children learn to expect. Several of these appeared in the first share group I recorded on September 21, and many persisted throughout the year. In the following excerpt, Cindy fields, probably for the first time, standard questions from Jake, Abby, and Pat. She has just finished reading *Stop,* a predictable repeating story by Joy Cowley (1981).

Jake: What's your favorite page?

Cindy [*shows picture of the crash*]: I like this one myself.

Pat: Why do you like that one?

Cindy: I don't know but I just like it. Abby.

Abby: Why did you choose that book—because it was funny or something?

Cindy: I just wanted to choose these because . . . I don't know but . . . I really don't know what it is but I like to read these books.

It is interesting that Pat poses the first why? question in this string, asking Cindy to give a reason for her choice. Very quickly, children pick up this pattern, and either the presenter gives a reason without prompting or another student in the group asks the why? question. Similarly, Abby's question about choosing the book is one that students soon come to expect.

During my music room interview in December, I asked the group what comments or questions they expected after sharing. They came up with the following list.

- What's your favorite page? Why is that your favorite page?
- What's your least favorite page? Why is that your least favorite page?
- You're a good reader.
- Why did you decide to choose that book?

The questions in this list can all be good ones, but many teachers, I suspect, might grow to consider them tiresome substitutes for real questions. The first graders, in particular, often asked them in a singsong, playful voice, and it was clear that they were not particularly interested in the answers. I expected the questions to die out. I thought they would become as tedious to students as they were to Pat and me. But they persisted, not as the only set of questions, but as regular contributions to the group.

Why this persistence? Our problem with understanding it, I believe, stems from our assumption that six- and seven-year-olds buy into an adult model of asking questions, that they ask questions to resolve perplexities, seek information, explore motives. But do the students in these groups feel such a compelling need to know the reader's favorite page, day after day, week after week? I doubt it. Instead, they see the opportunity to ask a sanctioned question as a way of participating in the group. It is the asking that is central; the answer is of secondary importance, and they often don't listen to it. According to Pat, the formula questions are like a free pass that allows anyone to enter a conversation.

> I think it is important that everybody in the group—anybody—can get into the discussion on a given day. That has a lot to do with the sense of community that you build up. You have a few of these predictable comments and someone will kind of repeat them and then all of a sudden they will be more comfortable telling their own story. We have conversation starters, too. You go to a cocktail party and you're mingling with people and there are certain things you can say: "Hi!" "How are you?" "How've you been lately?" "Did you have a good winter?" There are certain things you can talk about that are safe, easy starters for you.

The importance of these free passes was particularly evident in Melanie's case. For several weeks, she seemed lost and unnaturally quiet in the sharing groups. Her first question was, "What's your favorite page?" She had used her free pass.

The potential for asking formula questions was increased dramatically by a question-posing strategy introduced to the class by Billy. While it is usually impossible to trace the source of formula questions, the multiple-question strategy was, by all accounts, Billy's creation. At first, a child would be recognized to make *a* comment or ask *a* question; if the child wanted to continue, he or she would need to be recognized again by the book presenter. Billy, however, began to preface his turns with "I have two" or "I have three"—thus holding the floor for multiple questions. There was some disagreement about the maximum number of consecutive turns Billy had ever claimed. Jimmy, usually scrupulous in these matters, asserted

Billy once did "I have five." Billy, perhaps anxious to embellish his status, claimed to have once done "I have nine."

Billy's strategy was used primarily by the first graders in the class, who often took a more playful approach to the sharing groups. The challenge of the multiple-question strategy was not to think up good questions but to remember all of the formula questions one had promised to ask, not always an easy task. Here is Billy in an early exchange with Jimmy.

Billy: I have . . . why . . . I have a few. Why . . . What's your favorite page?

Jimmy: Well, there aren't much picture pages in this but it's this one. I like it. The picture—

Billy [*interrupting*]: And why is that your favorite page?

Jimmy: Well, one reason—

Billy [*interrupting*]: And you're a good reader.

Jimmy: Well, I do like . . . well, I don't like . . . well, I just like it because they're pictures in the story.

Billy: And you're a good reader.

Jimmy was probably on his way to answering the first question, but Billy cut him off because, had Jimmy added the explanation, Billy's questioning pattern would have been disrupted. Similarly, Billy begins his comment "You're a good reader" before Jimmy has answered the why? question. Pat commented on the exchange, "It's hard to listen when you've got a 'few' comments and questions on your mind."

According to Billy and Michelle, two first graders who used the "I have . . . " strategy frequently, some presenters evaded their questions unfairly. Billy complained about being skipped.

Billy: That happened to me once. See, Susan was sharing. I asked, "Why is that your favorite page?" She didn't answer. She said, "Allan." Then he said, "Why is that your favorite page?" And she said, "Because there are lots of colors." She skipped me. She didn't answer my question.

Michelle: That must make you sad.

Even Jimmy, a second grader who dislikes the formula questions, admits that this treatment is unfair. There were, however, tricks that could be used to throw off the questioner. The next exchange occurred in May after Don had presented *The Stupids Step Out* (Allard and Marshall, 1977).

Jed: I have two. What's your favorite page?
Don: No, no, don't ask me that.
Jed: Well, I have three.
Don: Oh no. I don't have one. They're all funny.
Jed: OK, that takes care of my other one.
Don: I know. It was going to be why is that your favorite page.
Jed: And when they look in the mirror, I think that was kind of weird because they probably felt stupid.

Don threw Jed off by not having a favorite page, thus canceling out the standard why? question that he knew was coming. Still, Jed had the presence of mind to move on to his comment about the mirror.

If we are looking for adultlike discussions of books, these consecutive formula questions appear silly and irrelevant. But if we treat the first graders as a subculture in this classroom, the reasons for the popularity of Billy's invention are clearer. We are witnessing a game, a test of memory—can the student follow through with the three, or four, or five (or nine!) questions and comments? It is also a game of control, of holding the floor, in which the presenter must come back to the same person several times in succession.

Another way to understand this playful use of formula questions is to see them as an example of what Irving Goffman (1961) calls "under-life." According to Goffman, institutions like mental asylums, workplaces, and schools assign roles to those involved in them. In order to develop and maintain a sense of self, inmates (of all sorts) distance themselves from the assigned roles; "the self is formed in the distance one takes from the roles one is assigned" (Brooke, 1987, 144). This underlife often takes the form of mild subversion that does not radically challenge the institution (e.g., identity jokes in a mental hospital) but does announce that the individual is more than the role assigned. Such subversions are not pathological but profoundly healthy—"only a fanatic completely associates himself with only one role" (144).

41

The institutional role for Billy and other participants in groups was that of serious questioner, seeker of information. That's the model that Pat had provided. But Billy inventively turned this expectation into a game that had nothing to do with seeking information. Questioning became a mildly subversive game of holding the floor through memorizing a set of questions. This is what Goffman calls a "contained" disruption because it doesn't really threaten the discussion; nevertheless, it allowed Billy to distance himself (as he often did) from the serious student role that Pat had demonstrated. Pat accepts such subversions as necessary if adult and child cultures are to interact.

As appealing as these formula questions were, the participants in the groups often modified and sharpened them—particularly the generic "favorite page" question. They developed several variations.

- What's your favorite word?
- Which did you think was the funniest page [in *Funnybones*]? (Ahlberg, 1981)
- What's your favorite thing that Mrs. Green did [in *The Teacher from the Black Lagoon*]? (Thaler, 1989)
- What's the scariest part [in *Arthur's Tooth*]? (Brown, 1985)
- What's your favorite country?
- What's your favorite funniest thing that happened in the book [*The Stupids Die*]? (Allard and Marshall, 1981)
- Who's your favorite *Stupids* character?
- Who's your favorite person?
- What's your favorite animal?

In one class, Martin shared *People* (Spier, 1980), a book filled with facts and pictures about different cultures. Rob asked him about gods.

Rob: Which god do you like best?
Martin: You mean in here?
Rob: Yeah.
Pat: Which what?
Rob: God.
Pat: God.

Rob: This one kind of looks neat.

Martin: I don't know anything about these gods so I really don't know.

Children in the class also helped expand the repertoire of questions. Megan, in particular, developed a type of question that became a standard in the class. It asked the presenter to imagine himself or herself in the story, variants of "If you could be anybody in that story, who would you be?"

I only ask that question sometimes, in sort of pretend books with maybe a chicken or wolf. I like asking that question because if I was going to do a play I would know what to ask people to do.

In fact, the question was asked about a variety of books. After Michelle read *The Easter Bunny's Lost Egg* (Gordon, 1980), Joyce (Megan's reading partner) asked, "If you were the Easter Bunny, where would you hide the eggs?" After Cindy had read Pete Seeger's *Abiyoyo* (1985), there was this exchange.

Joyce: If you had a magic wand like [one of the characters in the story], what do you think you would do with it? To get rid of . . .

Cindy: I would try to get rid of maybe my brother sometimes. If he's bothering me. But if he's being nice I wouldn't.

And when Phillip shared a personalized Christmas book that belonged to his friend Tommy, the following exchange took place.

Jimmy: Would you like to be in that book?

Phillip: Yeah. Tommy told me I could sit in the back with another Allan, not the one in our class. I'm sitting over there [*gestures toward picture*]. The different Allan is sitting over there. And Tommy is going to sit in front.

Jimmy: The Tommy Express [he had just shared Chris Van Allsburg's *The Polar Express* (1985)].

43

Given the way many children wrote their fiction in this class, Megan's question was very natural. They were constantly placing their friends in the fictional worlds they created in their writing, so to imagine themselves in texts was a very congenial thing to do.

Another ritual in the classroom was turning to the back of a book and reciting, sometimes in a chorus of two or three, the names of other books by the author. This pattern began early in the year.

Scott [*referring to the back of the book*]: Did you ever read *Clifford's Christmas, Clifford's Family, Clifford's Kitten, Clifford's Riddles, Clifford's ABC's,* or *Clifford's Sticker Book* [all books by Norman Bridwell]?

Pat: Those are all ones they list on the back?

Scott: Yeah. *Clifford's Sticker Book* is a sticker book.

Pat: Have you read any of the other ones there?

Scott: Yep. *Clifford's Christmas.*

Pat: Is that on the list?

Don: Yeah, every one is.

Scott: Yeah. *Clifford's Family.*

Don: Clifford's Kitten.

And they start on the list again. Often the children would treat this oral listing as a kind of roll call and come in with "I have that one." "I've read that one."

In October of the next school year, I stopped at Mast Way to drop off a form for Pat. It was Halloween week, and Abby's mother, Catherine, had brought in an elaborately carved pumpkin. It had been transformed into a haunted house with a witch, skeleton, cat, and lacy spider webs on two of the window panes, all lit by the orange glow of the candle. Catherine sat in the Author's Chair and told about carving these pumpkins as a child. She said that the secret to making the spider webs and other detailed cuts was to use a long knife with a very small blade.

The children sat around and listened, many of the girls right at Catherine's feet, the boys spread throughout the area. It was strange to look out at Cindy, Michelle, Jed, Scott, and Abby (so proud of her mother's work) and to think that they were now the mighty second graders and the cycle had begun again, without me. And without Billy. He was in another second-grade class. The room seemed a little subdued without his brand of craziness.

After Catherine had spoken, it was time for questions and comments. Children raised their hands—"How long did it take?" "Is it hard to do?" "What's the hardest part?" Almost all of them were totally attentive, but at the back of the room, sitting by himself, was a first grader who looked like a little Billy (though he was not related). He fidgeted like Billy and seemed to stare off into space, into that dimension that first-grade boys write about. He had his hand up, though he seemed to be looking out the window.

Catherine pointed to him. "Andy. Andy."

The boy looked away from the window but still not at Catherine, "Um, um, I have three."

Billy's invention lives on.

4

Amen

IN FEBRUARY, ABBY opened her sharing turn with this introduction to her book.

This is *Lazy Lions and Lucky Lambs* by Patricia Reilly Giff [1985]. It's mostly about two boys named Matthew and Richard and they always get into trouble. You see in the first picture he thinks he can walk with his eyes closed all the way to his sister Holly's room. She is in the fifth grade and he pretends he has a message so he has a reason to be there, but he doesn't say anything to Holly. He whispers in her ear, but he doesn't say anything and the teacher gets mad.

And in another room picture, here they are. It's not in the room. They are fighting on a snowpile at recess which you're not allowed to do. And so Miss K., the strictest teacher, sends them to the principal's office. They keep saying they're not going to do it again and they're not going to get into trouble. But they do.

Listening to Abby talk about books was a little like watching her run at recess. Sometimes, just for the pleasure of it, I would ask, "Abby, would you run to the swing set and back?" She always agreed. She had long legs for a first grader and seemed to glide effortlessly, as if she was not in a big hurry. Only when someone was running beside her (or behind her) was it possible to gauge her swiftness.

Like her running, Abby's introduction seemed effortless. No pauses or "ums" or backtracking. She begins by orienting her listeners: "It's mostly about two boys named Matthew and Richard and they always get into trouble." In this opening sentence, she provides us with a theme—getting into trouble—that helps us focus our attention. She then follows through by describing two occasions when the boys get into trouble at school.

Abby was also able to deal with a problem that derailed almost every student in the class at some point in the year: that of identifying characters as they appear in the summary. She might easily have mentioned "Holly" without identifying her as "his sister Holly" who is "in the fifth grade" (though we don't know if the "he" is Matthew or Richard). And when Miss K. sends the boys to the principal's office, Abby identifies her as "the strictest teacher." This explicit identification of characters is hard for students sharing books because they know who the characters are and forget that others might not.

Abby's achievement becomes more apparent if we allow someone to run beside her. Here is how Rob summarized his book, *The Sign of the Beaver,* by Elizabeth Speare (1984):

> It's about a boy named Mat and his father went away to get his wife and baby. And he asked could he have the wagon that could fit three so Mat couldn't come so he stayed in the cabin and then he stays there and he . . . his father . . . and then one day Mat . . . I mean this guy named . . . I think his name was Claude and he came and gave Mat some bear stew or something like that. And then Mat went to sleep . . . and the only weapon that Mat had was a gun so he killed animals but then Claude stole the gun and then when Mat woke up in the morning he thought it was a bear.

Rob continued his summary for another minute or two, but by this point we were confused because of missing information. Why did the father have to ask permission to use the wagon? Who did he ask? Who is Claude? A friend? If so, why did he steal the gun? What did Mat mistake for a bear? Rob, it should be noted, is a competent second-grade reader, but the challenge of both remembering the complex plot of his book and providing background information for listeners was almost overwhelming. And, while I realize that some hierarchies of thinking place summarizing at a low level, I wonder if those who construct these hierarchies have listened to the struggles of children like Rob.

Transforming, Not Duplicating

"Could you tell us something about the book before you start reading it." Even well into the year, Pat had to insert this reminder into the book discussions. The first graders, especially, tended to skip over the summary and begin by reading aloud. In the beginning, I thought they simply forgot. But as I heard her gentle reminder again and again, I began to see that she was altering in a significant way the ideas of "reading" and "sharing" that these students brought to the group.

Many first graders, understandably, saw reading as a performance in decoding. To share a book, for them, was to share this performance of decoding by reading the book aloud to an audience. But Pat's gentle prompt to "say something about the book" pushed the students to do something new. They had to translate the author's words into their own, to give priority to their own language.

It is a deceptively revolutionary request—to share is not simply to duplicate the words of the author but to transform them. The German philosopher Hans-Georg Gadamer put it this way:

> To understand a text is to come to understand oneself in a kind of dialogue. This contention is confirmed by the fact that the concrete dealing with a text yields understanding only when what is said in the text begins to find expression in the interpreter's own language. (Quoted in Bartholomae, 1986, 90–91)

According to David Bartholomae, the real event of understanding often occurs when we "speak over" the words of the author. In their introductions, students were asked to "speak over" the texts.

When asked to "say something about the book," many of the children produced a chain narrative (see Applebee, 1978), a string of events connected by *and*. All of the incidents may have been accurately recalled, but there was little sense of story. An example is Vicky's account of Esther Averill's *The Fire Cat* (1960).

> Well, the cat [*ten-second pause*] a girl finds him and um Pickles climbs up a tree and saves a cat and then the police come and give him a fire hat and Pickles is a firecat.

Michelle was more successful with her summary of *The Easter Bunny's Lost Egg* by Sharon Gordon (1980):

> The book is about the Easter Bunny hides some eggs and um he lost his last egg and then he was going to sit under a tree and he sat on his last Easter Egg and he said, "Oh, that's where I hid the last Easter Egg."

Michelle's ability to quote the final line directly was both impressive and atypical for first graders.

51

Some students simplified the task and did not give summaries, instead locating incidents that they wanted to share. This was perfectly acceptable in Pat's eyes, as when Jennifer was sharing *The Night Before Christmas* and Pat had to intercept her before she began to read.

Jennifer: This is called *The Night Before Christmas* by Clement Moore. "'Twas the night—"

Pat: Um, could you tell us a little about it first?

Jennifer: Well, uh, I like the part when he laughs it looks like a bowlful of jelly. Then he says . . . it sort of reminds me when the "stockings are hanging by the chimney with care" I don't have mine hanging by the chimney because the chimney is in my mom's closet.

Donald used the same incident-focused introduction when he talked about *The Stupids Step Out* (Allard and Marshall, 1977).

It's about these stupid people and like they do all these funny things like the mother wears the cat as a hat and like they go in the bathtub and the sister says, "But where's the water?" and the father says, "Don't be stupid we don't want our clothes to get wet." So they just get in and there's no water. And the shampoo is jam or tunafish.

Another fairly obvious way that the presenters kept their summaries on track was to use the pictures as a cue to remembering the text. Adam used this approach when he shared Chris Van Allsburg's *Two Bad Ants* (1988). As you read what Adam said, imagine the book pages being turned.

The *Two Bad Ants* by Chris Van Allsburg. And it's about a scout that . . . an ant scout that came home with a crystal piece of sugar and the Queen Ant liked it so much she demanded a hundred scouts go out and they say that the grass was woods and it got darker and darker and soon they came to a wall and they started climbing up but it looked like a cliff, a mountain cliff, and then they went to a crack in the window and then they landed on the table where you know there was sort of like this size of cup [*indicating coffee cup on the table*] of sugar but to them it was humongous and the two little ants decided to stay there and munch on it. And they went to sleep and then they woke up when somebody had to have sugar to put in their coffee and they got lifted up and dropped into the coffee.

He went on for a couple more minutes, summarizing the action of several picture pages.

Without the support of the pictures, though, summarizing long picture books and sections from chapter books is difficult for children this age, and Pat must decide whether she will ask questions to clarify summaries. I raised this issue in connection with Sandy's summary of *Arthur's Valentine* (Brown, 1985).

It's about when Arthur . . . he was getting ready to go outside when Violet was making him a valentine. And Arthur decided he'd have a snowball fight by himself. But then Violet said that he can't and Arthur made a snowball fight by himself. But it made a big spot in front of him and he forgot to climb under it and so when he practiced Wilma was coming down the path and invited them to her Valentine's party. And then this other snowball hit her on the head and then in the middle of the book Arthur gave a valentine to Norman but they used to be friends but when Arthur was playing in the school Norman fell down on the ground and tore his new jacket so they weren't friends anymore.

In the transcript that I passed on to Pat, I wrote, "Pat, I have real trouble following Sandy. Do you ever ask students questions about these oral summaries?" Pat wrote back:

I think I was following Sandy a little better than you because I knew the story and I knew the part she was telling about. Reading over the transcript I think I might have asked her a few questions if I didn't know the book.

When they start to get into longer stories, these summaries become more difficult. Sometimes it helps them to think about a main event in the beginning, middle, and end of the story. I don't remember talking to Sandy about that but she tries that strategy for herself when she says, "in the middle of the book Arthur gave a valentine." Last year a couple of girls would bring their written summaries to the table and read them.

There was probably another reason for her sparing use of questions at this point: Pat is generally reluctant to be the first questioner and prefers to allow students to establish a pattern before she speaks. If she comes in with several clarifying questions early on, other members of the group might easily defer to her as the primary questioner. She could easily fall into the swamp of initiate-respond-evaluate.

Selecting and Planning

In order for there to be discussion about each book, the reader often has to select a part of the book to share, and this planning is very difficult for many children. It was typical, early in the year, for a first grader to read until Pat gently interrupted: "Have you planned how much you are going to share with us? Because we need time for questions and comments." Because young children see reading as a performance of a whole, it often takes them a while to figure out how to read only part of a book. For example, in October, Jake was still unsure about how much he could share.

Jake: I can't read the title.

Pat: Spectacles [Raskin, 1968].

Jake: Should I read the whole book or what?

Pat: I doubt you'll have enough time for the whole book if I remember right [*looks at book*]. Well, you might have enough time. I can't tell for sure [*continues looking*]. No, you probably won't have enough time for the whole book, but you'd have enough time for four or five pages.

Pat placed considerable emphasis on the child being able to plan a sharing turn. She wrote, "In some ways I think this ability to

54

plan ahead—to think about what they want to share—is a sign of maturity." We can see this ability in Tommy's introduction to his book, *Arthur's April Fool* (Brown, 1985).

> My book is *Arthur's April Fool* and I'm going to read the funny parts up to the end, the funny parts near the end. I'll read the funny parts up to the end and it's about Arthur. Well, Binky Barnes takes Arthur's pencil so Arthur takes a telescope to him and he said, "You can see something you've never seen before and if you give me back my pencil I'll write it." But it's so difficult he had to put it backwards so Binky put it to the mirror and it said, "April Fool."

Just as with Abby's summary of *Lazy Lions and Lucky Lambs,* it is easy to miss the achievement of this introduction. Tommy let his audience know that he planned to share an episode near the end. Then, in a few lines, he was (almost) able to describe the trick that Arthur pulls. Unlike other summaries, Tommy's also explained *why* the action occurs—why Arthur is tricking Binky. And, like Michelle, Tommy inserted dialogue from the story into his summary. The only possible confusion arose when he referred to the difficulty with the backward message (because the telescope lenses invert the image.) In Pat's eyes, Tommy's summary represented an impressive piece of planning.

Students also demonstrated their ability to plan by summarizing their stories up to the point where they would begin reading, thus synchronizing summary and oral reading. We can see this strategy in Megan's summary of Eric Carle's *Pancakes, Pancakes* (1990).

> This book is about a boy and he wakes up very hungry and he wants a large pancake for breakfast and he goes downstairs and he asks his mother. He says, "May I have a large pancake for breakfast." And his mothers says he can but he has to help her. And he gets all these things to help her. He gets some wheat from the field and he goes to the mill and he gets some flour from it. And he gets an egg from a black hen. And he gets milk from a cow. And then he makes butter from the milk. And this is where I'm going to start sharing.

Blurring the Boundaries

When I graduated from college in 1970, Jesse Jackson gave the commencement speech. It was a wonderful speech, by turns angry, funny, ironic, idealistic. He was preaching to us, yet the cadences, the rhythm of the repetitions were utterly different from the dry exposition of the Presbyterian sermons I had endured as a child. We listened, rapt, ready to applaud him loudly when he finished. But in the middle of his speech, he broke off, looked down at us, and said, "What's the matter with you? Isn't somebody going to say 'amen' or something?"

Well, no. That wasn't the way most of us were brought up. The preacher in our church held the floor. We could laugh at the (infrequent) funny parts, but we couldn't talk or comment while the speaker spoke. The dividing line was clear. If we commented at all, it was after the sermon, usually on the way home from church. To interject our voices into Jesse Jackson's speech seemed out of line, a violation of the norms we had been raised to respect. As I recall, somebody did let out a weak "amen," but for the rest of Jackson's speech we indicated agreement only by nodding our heads—until the end, of course, when we gave him a standing ovation.

At the beginning of my year at Mast Way, discussions followed a compartmentalized model with the "questions and comments" section clearly separate from the oral reading of the story. Commentary followed performance, just as our applause followed Jesse's speech. Initially, the only pauses in the oral reading occurred when the reader didn't know a word and asked someone else in the group for help. Then, around the middle of the year, things changed. Instead of waiting for the book to be finished, members of the group jumped in without raising their hands, commenting on the book *as it was read*. They kibitzed. They pointed out what they saw in the pictures. They repeated the words of the book. Finally, when the reading was done, there would be something ironic in the ritualistic call for "comments and questions." The commenting had been going on all along.

The key to this shift was, I believe, the familiarity and popularity of some books (like those in the *Arthur* series). When the children all knew the book, they could all chime in with their own observations and embellishments. (Families know and retell their stories in much the same way.) And, in fact, research indicates that student comments increase with repeated readings (Morrow, 1988). Familiarity (up to a point) fosters rather than deadens response. This seemed to be the case in Pat's class at midyear.

The children also knew each other better, and the readiness to participate in the turn of a peer, even to co-narrate the peer's story, was a sign of membership in a friendship group. As you read the following extended transcript, imagine the voices continually jumping in on one another, sharing in Rob's turn. Imagine a good time.

Rob: I'm going to share *The Stupids Die* by Harry Allard and it's about this Stupids family and they do crazy stuff like Buster mows the rug. Petunia waters the house plants.

Don: With a sprinkler.

Rob: And the clocks are all messed up.

Don: Bong, bong, bong, bong, bong [*referring to a picture*]. He's swinging on it.

Jed: Let me see.

Rob: And Buster's eating with his feet. And, and—

Jed: What's the picture say?

Rob: The Stupids mother and father say that he's learning manners.

Scott: Then why aren't they eating with their feet?

Rob continued his summary for another couple minutes with Don helping with the narration. Jed and Scott, the two first graders in the group, play different roles: Jed comments appreciatively on the pictures, and Scott questions the internal logic of the story. Pat says nothing.

Rob [*reading*]: "One morning Stanley Q. Stupid woke up with a funny feeling. 'Something really stupid is going to happen today,' he said.

'Oh, wow,' said the two Stupid kids. The Stupids all had breakfast in the shower, as usual. 'My eggs are all runny,' said Mr. Stupid."

Don [*laughing*]: The shower. Eggs.

Scott: But it's impossible 'cause he's not in the . . . He's not in the . . .

Rob: He's not getting wet.

Jed: Rob, can you show the pictures? You forget about the pictures.

Rob [*showing the picture*]: That one and that one.

Jed: He's not getting wet—just the kids and the mother, especially the mother.

Rob: The mother, yeah. [*He laughs then continues reading.*] "After breakfast the two Stupid kids had chores to do. Buster mowed the rug."

Don: I wouldn't be on the rug.

Jed: Oh my God, he's mowing it so it's—

Rob: "And Petunia watered all the houseplants."

Jed and Don: With a sprinkler.

Scott: But it never grows back up again.

Jed: Yes it does. Because they move again.

Rob [*reading*]: "Bong Bong Bong Bong Bong [*Jed joins in.*] Bong Bong Bong Bong Bong Bong The clock in the hall struck eleven. 'Noon,' cried Mr. Stupid. 'Time for lunch!' "

Don: It's not noon. Look at the clock. It says three seven.

Jed: Can I do the numbers?

Don: It says three seven.

Jed: I like the "bong, bong, bong, bong."

This transcript shows one advantage of multiage grouping. I always pictured Jed, in this and other groups, as the younger brother, tagging along, trying to fit in. One way of fitting in was to join the unofficial club that Rob and Don had formed, call it the Stupids club. Jed was banging at the door. And the way to get in was to read the book.

In the case of *The Stupids Die,* the commentary was primarily an appreciation of the book's humor, particularly the visual humor (e.g., mowing the carpet). In the following discussion, in which Abby shared *Hot Air Henry* (Calhoun, 1981), the commentary is more speculative. After her summary, she began to read:

Abby: Hot Air Henry. "Henry wanted to fly with everyone. Everybody in his family had gone up with the balloon. But the man always declared, 'I'm not flying with that cat.' "

Phillip: The cat would probably jump out.

Jimmy: They're just showing that *that* man does not like *that* cat.

Pat: He doesn't, does he?

Michelle: He hates it.

Abby [*reading the section where the balloon is filled with hot air and Henry leaps into the basket*]: "One of his claws snagged on the cord that fired the balloon. There was a horrible roar. 'Grab that cat,' yelled the man. The kid runs for Henry and slipped on the snow. The burner kept roaring. The flames heated the air. And up went the balloon. Up went Henry. Up, up, and away. Henry was flying."

Phillip: Oh, and he hit the button?

Michelle: What made him go up so fast?

As Abby read on, the group commented in a number of ways. Jimmy asked how the cat learned how to fly.

Abby: I think just from watching.

Michelle: Yeah, he doesn't have a plane.

Michelle and Phillip imagine themselves as Henry.

Phillip: If I was that cat I would do that. No I wouldn't. I'm scared of hot air.

Michelle: I'm not scared.

And Michelle played with the word *yoyo* after hearing the bit where Henry bounces to the ground and says, "I'm not a yoyo."

Michelle: Yoyo. Yoyo. Yoyo. My dad's good at yoyos. I'm horrible at yoyos.

In all, there were twenty-seven comments during Abby's reading, and, rather than derailing her, they served to indicate the intense interest of Jimmy, Phillip, and Michelle.

In virtually all of the running commentaries, pictures figured more centrally than the text because, in most picture books, the illustrations are far more elaborate than the text. Sometimes it was as if the students tried to squeeze as much information as they could out of the illustrations—they milked the pictures. This was another example of the six- and seven-year-old culture at work, the same culture that can spend hours poring over *Waldo* books. (As I write, three of the top four books on the *New York Times* "Miscellaneous and Self-help" bestsellers list are books from Martin Handford's *Waldo* series.)

The following excerpt from a discussion of *Arthur's Nose* (Brown, 1976) is one of many examples of milking the picture. In the book, Arthur, an anteater, is self-conscious about his nose (which would be a problem if you were an anteater). The final part of the excerpt relates to the part of the book where Arthur goes to the rhinologist and has a chance to choose from a variety of other noses.

Jed: The name of this book is *Arthur's Nose* by Marc Brown. And he's worried about his nose and he wants to change his nose because he's worried about it and he goes to this place but he doesn't change his nose and Francine says, "I still want to change my seat at school." Because his nose is always dripping and bothering her. This is Arthur's house. [*He reads.*]

Vicky: Wow, that was probably the first book.

Jed: I know.

Vicky: It tells about their family.

Jed [*reading and then stopping at the picture of Arthur's running nose*]: I don't think his nose looks that funny because my nose looks like that. [*He starts reading again.*]

Jake: Achooo.

Jed: It doesn't say "achoo."

Sandy: Picture, picture.

Jed: I think Francine is making a little model of his nose.

Pat: Yeah.

Vicky: And with purple clay. I thought he had a brown nose.

Jed [*reading*]: Look at his sharp fingernails.

Vicky: Wow.

Adam: Oh, my God.

Sandy: It looks like pencil sharpeners sharpened them. [*Jed continues reading.*]

Vicky: Can I see the noses?

Adam: Picture, picture.

Vicky: I've got to see these noses. Elephant.

Jake: Fish.

Adam: Where's the emu?

Vicky: Where's the fish? Where's the fish?

Jake: Emu, right here.

Sandy: A fish.

Vicky: Where's the fish, Jed?

Jed: The fish is right there.

Vicky: No way, I think the mouth is too big.

And so for three or four minutes they crowded around *Arthur's Nose,* called out for the pictures to be shown around ("Picture, picture"), and speculated on the nose Arthur might have chosen.

Sessions like this one also provide an answer to the question, how can children share in these groups if they can't read, if they don't even know the letters yet? The question itself implies an adult definition of what a text is. For many of these children—even the competent readers—the interest is not primarily in the written words but in the story and the pictures. A child who has heard a book read can approximate the text (what Ellen Blackburn [1984] calls "invented reading") and show the pictures. Or a child can share a wordless book, telling the story. What can the child share? The picture. The picture.

Many Marx Brothers movies open at some excessively stuffy formal gathering—a reception (*Animal Crackers*), the speech of a college president (*Horsefeathers*), an opera (*A Night at the Opera*), a coronation (*Duck Soup*). The event is usually presided over by the wonderfully obtuse Margaret Dumont. Enter the Marx Brothers, and the event unravels—Groucho sings "Lydia the Tatooed Lady," Harpo chases young women, and Dumont tries futilely to maintain decorum ("Captain Spaulding, if you pleeease!").

The comparison doesn't quite work. Pat is no Margaret Dumont. But like these movies, the share groups begin formally, ritualistically. There is an understood order for the sharing group. There is the raising of hands, the calling on speakers. But if the group is to move beyond this formality, the structure must be subverted, the boundaries blurred. The more disruptive, associational, more humorous six- and seven-year-old culture must enter in. Pat watches as the formalities crumble.

She is, I believe, on Groucho's side.

5

The Tooth Fairy Doesn't Write Cursive

ONE EVENING, WHILE walking the dog with me, my son looked up at the stars to locate Mars, the brightest star in the sky, his wishing star. He explained, "One night I wished for the Wildcats [the University of New Hampshire hockey team] to win, and they did. And the next night I wished for the Bruins to win, and they did. And then I wished for the Wildcats to win again, and they did." Then he paused, "You know, Dad, I think stars are reusable."

Reusable wishing stars. This mix of logic and fantasy is characteristic of children's talk as they try to determine, in Jimmy's words, what is "really real." According to Howard Gardner (1978), children at this age are emerging from the preschool period where fantasy and reality are inseparably combined.

> Subjected daily to an assortment of relatives, monsters, historic persons, fairy tale characters, and puppets, the child cannot reliably determine how real (or unreal) each of these figures might be. Indeed the whole notion of what is real and what is fantastic is too complex for the child to grasp. As a consequence, the preschool child is forever uncertain about whether a witch might really devour her, whether a parent might suddenly disappear, whether Santa Claus has the same status as the milkman, the president, the Easter Bunny, or God. (340–41)

At about age six, children begin to sort out the "really real." According to my son, the Tooth Fairy is not real. The same for the Easter Bunny ("it would take too big a rabbit"). Santa Claus is real but not as real as George Washington because he is "in history." At other times, he is less sure—"Santa is fifty-fifty."

In her wonderful book, *Wally's Stories* (1981), Vivian Paley records conversations in which children sort out the reality of their worlds. In the following excerpt, they explore the issue of wishing on the man in the moon.

Earl: My cousin says you can wish on the man in the moon. I told my mother and she said it's only pretend.
Wally: He doesn't have a face or a body.
Lisa: Then he can't see. He's not real.
Deana: But how could he get in?

Wally: With a drill.

Eddie: The moon won't break. It's white like a ghost. The drill would pass in but no hole would come out.

Earl: There can't be a moon man because there's no door. How could he get in?

Eddie brings up the topic of the astronauts who walked on the moon and carried oxygen but agrees that a moon man would have to find a door. He also observes that the astronauts had to go to the moon when it was whole, otherwise they would be cut in half. But, according to Warren, the moon man can squeeze in half.

Wally: That's what I said. He's a round shape or a half round shape. But I never saw a door.

Eddie: There's no air there. No air! But air is invisible so how can there be no air?

Wally: Only the moon man sees it. He makes himself invisible so he can see it.

Earl: My cousin says you can wish on him.

Wally: The moon is right next to God so he could talk to God. (63–64)

Since, in the cosmology of five-year-olds, God has the greatest power (followed by fairies, Santa Claus, and magicians, in that order), being next to God was good evidence for the potency of the man in the moon.

In the book discussions in Pat's class, there were vestiges of this kind of reality testing, often focusing on the Tooth Fairy. One book that invariably set the class off on tooth stories was *Arthur's Tooth* (Brown, 1985). At first, this discussion focused on blood— Jimmy claimed that the illustrations should show blood where Arthur's tooth had come out. The discussion then moved on to the Tooth Fairy.

Martin: When my tooth fell out I didn't even know it and I couldn't even find it so I had to write a note to the Tooth Fairy and I put it under my pillow and I still got half a dollar for it.

Pat: Even though you didn't have the tooth there.

Martin: Yeah.

Megan: I lost a tooth once and I really lost it and I wrote a note to the Tooth Fairy and the next morning I did find a dollar under my pillow but I also found my tooth under the pillow.

Pat: Ohh. Did the Tooth Fairy explain how the tooth turned up under the pillow? [*Megan indicates no.*]

Megan, Martin, and, later on, Jimmy are second graders who play along with the Tooth Fairy game. But Billy is still on the edge of belief.

Billy [*excitedly*]: Well, I know because the Tooth Fairy doesn't know. I know it was my mom because the Tooth Fairy doesn't know I practice the violin.

Pat [*laughing*]: So how is that connected?

Jimmy: The Tooth Fairy might.

Pat: So why? Did she leave a note for you?

Billy: Yeah. It was my mom. She wrote it. The Tooth Fairy I don't think writes in cursive.

Jimmy: You never know.

At times, they argued logically for the existence of Santa Claus and the Easter Bunny. In one discussion, Jennifer asked Tommy, point-blank, if he believed in Santa Claus.

Tommy. No.

Vicky: I do. I believe in Santa Claus 'cause I know my mother and my father wouldn't spend $300 on me.

Evan: Yeah. I know my mother wouldn't buy a Nintendo and I got a Nintendo.

Later in the discussion, Nathan used the same logic to argue for the Easter Bunny.

Nathan: I believe in the Easter Bunny because my mom and dad wouldn't go downstairs in the middle of the night and go out to the stores 'cause the stores are closed.

Abby: Well, they could go when you're at school.

Nathan: Yeah. Well, they do give you some stuff, but there's other stuff too.

The arguments of Nathan, Evan, and Vicky can easily be reduced to the classical syllogism: (1) If my parents were *x,* they would have to do *y;* (2) my parents would never do *y;* (3) therefore, my parents are not *x.* Logic and fantasy fused.

At times, the members of the groups laughed at the non-realistic perspectives of their younger siblings. Rob, for example, noted that his younger brother thought that daddy longlegs made their webs by pulling off and arranging their long legs. On the subject of ghosts, however, the class was divided. For example, Abby tried to laugh at the naïveté of one of her sister's classmates who believed in ghosts, only to find that Sandy, a second grader, shared that belief.

Abby: There's a boy in my sister's class and his name is Jerrod. She is in kindergarten and people believe in ghosts and so one day he said he saw a ghost when he was a little kid [*she giggles*].

Sandy: Ghosts are true.

Jake: They are. They are.

Sandy: They are. Dead people. Dead people come alive. Dead people come alive. But they're ghosts. I never saw a ghost in my life though.

Abby: There are no such thing as ghosts.

While Sandy believes in ghosts, she stops short of making the claim that Jerrod made—of actually seeing a ghost.

As Gardner indicated in his observation about fantasy in children's lives, a number of phenomena fall somewhere between the fantastic and the real. Mexican jumping beans, for example. In a discussion of *George and Martha Back in Town* (Marshall, 1984), the conversation switched to Rob's recollection of a scene in another story in which George claims to be a snake charmer (snake charming would also be in that middle, semifantastic range). It then moved to Martin's Mexican jumping beans:

Martin: I have some Mexican jumping beans.

Rob: But they don't jump.

Martin: They just go like that [*indicates a rolling motion*]. I looked for Mexican jumping beans and I finally found one and there was a little bug in one of the Mexican jumping beans that was cracked and it was dead. And that's how Mexican jumping beans jump.

Pat: Because there's a little insect inside.

Cindy [*the book presenter*]: Rob.

Rob: I got some Mexican jumping beans and they jump so much. They jump so high and went so far. And one time I put them on my desk and they were in a box and when they jumped the box top opened and they jumped out of the box.

Pat: They really jumped?

Rob: Yeah.

Pat: They really jumped instead of wiggling around?

Rob: Yeah. It jumped.

Martin: Must have been pretty strong insects.

Pat's comment on this interchange: "Martin wouldn't accuse his good friend of fibbing."

Martin was in a delicate position. Rob's account was at odds with his own carefully observed, scientifically explained experience with jumping beans. Doubting the story that Rob told but unwilling to accuse his friend of lying, he graciously allowed Rob to save face with his comment, "Must have been pretty strong insects."

A more interesting question is, why would Rob stretch the truth as he did, given the class norms of truth telling? The answer has to do with the ways in which boys in the class took "strong turns." The rule for strong turns can be stated like this: in a discussion of the fantastic, the weird, the gross, or the stupid, you must better, in some way improve on, the account that went before; otherwise, you seem only to tag along with "That happened to me, too." There was an element of one-upmanship in the discussion: Martin's beans rolled; Rob's jumped clear out of the box. Had it been someone else—perhaps Billy—Martin might have been more openly skeptical. But Rob was his friend.

Testing World Knowledge

Just as snake charmers and Mexican jumping beans occupy the mid-range of reality, much of the fiction children read is neither "really real" nor fantasy. Some books, like Joanna Cole's *Magic Schoolbus* series, blend the true and the imaginary. Paradoxically, these fictional books may be better for exploring reality than books that are clearly informational. Whereas children learn from books that are clearly factual and "true," they test the reality of books that are fictional. They apply their knowledge of the physical world and human behavior to determine if descriptions and actions are plausible. They ask, "Could this really happen?" "Would I act this way?"

One book that regularly starts a discussion on spiders is Eric Carle's *A Very Busy Spider* (1989), which Corrine had shared with the group. In the book, a spider constructing a web ignores the diverting invitations of a variety of animals. Pat asked, "So in the whole book the spider never says anything?"

Corrine: Uh-huh.

Megan: But all the other animals do.

Pat: But all the other animals have their voices?

Megan: But the spider doesn't say anything.

Pat: But does the spider have a voice?

Megan: Well.

Pat: Have you ever heard a spider?

Megan: No.

Adam: Charlotte's Web.

Pat: Yeah. *Charlotte's Web.*

Megan: I think spiders do probably have a way of talking to each other.

Joyce: I learned that when another spider wants to come onto the web they have a special thing that they tap on the web when they come in so that they know it's not a bug.

Pat: So when there's a spider web and another spider wants to come on they tap on the web—

Joyce: A special way.

Pat: A special way.

Joyce: Yeah.

Pat: So they communicate more by feeling than by talking, by voice.

Although the capacity to test the realism of stories did not break exactly along grade lines (as we will see later, Scott was a skillful critic), it did seem more the province of the second graders, particularly Megan and Jimmy. In a sharing turn on *The Easter Bunny's Lost Egg* (Gordon, 1980), a repeating story book shared by Michelle, a first grader, Megan raised a question about whether an egg could be hidden "under a rock."

Megan: Wouldn't the Easter egg break if you hid it under a rock?

Michelle: No, if the rock rolled over it would break.

Megan: No, in the book it said, "He hid one under a rock." And if he hid one under a rock then wouldn't the egg break?

Michelle: No because he hid it in the side of the rock.

The issue of realism is deceptively complex in this short exchange. Michelle believes in the Easter Bunny; Megan does not. Megan accepts the fictional world in which the Easter Bunny exists, but she insists (gently) that this fictional world should obey the rules of physical causation as she understands them. A rock would crush an Easter egg.

This skepticism can lead to negativity as second graders see stories falling short of their new standards of plausibility. Jimmy seemed to cross this line in his criticism of Allan's published "The Detectives" (though Allan was not in the group when it was shared).

Jimmy [*noting that the clothes change color from one page to the next*]: How in the world can you change clothes in a second?

Vicky: Yeah, how can they change their clothes?

Jimmy: In just one second they did it. [*Vicky turns to the next page.*]

71

Jimmy: How in the world could they change again?

Sandy: What do you mean?

Jimmy: They changed clothes again.

Sandy: Oh yeah.

Vicky: In just one second. They're yellow right here and brown right there.

In a share group on *The Mystery of the Missing Red Mitten* (Kellogg, 1974), Jimmy commented on the line "A snowman with a heart," said by the boy when he finds his red mitten buried in the chest of his snowman. Jimmy objected, "I've never heard of such a thing. Snowmans are dead. They don't live. They are air. They are clouds. They are vapor."

We hear in comments like this the voice of the rationalist—snowmen are dead, Mexican jumping beans move because of a worm inside them, ghosts don't exist, it would take too big a rabbit to do the Easter Bunny's work. As adults, we mourn the loss of these beliefs, but I suspect that, for many children, the new rational theories liberate them, make them less passive.

One evening when I was coaching third base at a T-ball game, I asked the third baseman what his name was. He was bored with the game and happy to talk. "Max," he said.

I decided to go literary on him. "Max, what a great name. Max is the name of the boy in *Where the Wild Things Are*. I love that book."

"Yeah, they want to eat him up they love him so. And you know, I think it was a dream."

"Why is that?"

"Because his supper was still hot." He smiled at me and began digging a hole in the dirt with his toe.

Psychological Realism

In addition to theories about physical causation, children develop theories about human motivation that they use to test the narratives they read and hear. In a discussion of *Arthur's April Fool* (Brown, 1985), the talk inevitably moved to April Fool tricks that the children in the group had pulled. Tommy tells this story:

72

Tommy: I went to my dad. I said something like, "Get up." I said something like I want a toy for my birthday and he said, "Which kind of toy?" "A paper toy." And then he gave me a piece of paper. So I drew something and I told him to go to the store and find it. I knew he couldn't find it. And he came back to me and told me he couldn't find it. So I said, April Fool.

Pat: So you sent him on a chase for something he couldn't find.

Tommy: Uh-huh. Corrine.

Corrine [*a little shocked*]: So you sent him on a chase that wasn't real.

Tommy: Yeah.

Pat's comment on this exchange was, "Corrine asks again to be sure she understands. She probably doesn't think her dad would see the humor in that April Fool joke." Put another way, Tommy's story seemed implausible because it violated Corrine's sense of psychological causation (just as the Easter egg story violated Megan's sense of physical causation)—a father in this situation would be angry, not amused.

This reality testing also occurs when it comes to analyzing motives of characters in picture books. The following discussion took place after Allan shared *The Teacher from the Black Lagoon* (Thaler, 1989). In it, a boy has heard that his new teacher, Mrs. Green, is "a real monster." He sits in his empty classroom on the first day of school, and soon Mrs. Green comes in—and she *is* a real monster (she illustrates fractions by biting a student in half). After the story, as in my third-base conversation with Max, the talk focused on the reality of these monster scenes, and, typically, Jimmy began with "Do you think that could really happen in the real world?" Allan said, "No way." A couple of exchanges later, Scott came back to the question.

Scott: Well, I don't think that this happened. I think it was a dream.

Allan: I don't think so. Because it's his first day of school and I don't think he would be dreaming in school, on the first day of school.

73

Scott: Well, maybe that is his dream from his nap. . . .

Pat: Well, how do you think the story goes then? You don't think he was dreaming?

Allan: No.

Pat: How do you think all those ideas came to him about those teachers?

Allan: I don't know.

Pat: Who was telling him about those teachers? How did he find out?

Allan: I don't know. Well, at the picture I was drawing he's looking at a paper that tells all the teachers and what they have.

Pat: So he's the first one in the classroom.

Allan: Yeah.

Pat: All by himself.

Allan: Now I think he's dreaming.

Pat: What makes you think so?

Allan: Because he's closing his eyes.

Jimmy: And he dreams about all terrible things.

Allan's reason for resisting Scott's suggestion that the monster incidents are part of a dream is interesting. To Allan, it seemed implausible that a kindergartner or first grader, nervous about the teacher he would have, would fall asleep in class before school even began. Allan wouldn't act that way, and he had difficulty imagining that the boy would.

The testing of story worlds did not always take this skeptical turn. By projecting themselves into stories, they were also able to fantasize, to escape the realism of the world as it is, to view the narrative world as superior to the experienced world. During the sharing of *Teach Us, Amelia Bedelia* (Parish, 1987), a group of boys, led by Scott, imagined the pleasure of being in the classroom run by Amelia Bedelia. Scott began by counting recesses.

Scott: See they have one recess and then another one for "you go outside" and one before school—that's three recesses.

Martin: We have three recesses.

Scott: I know, but they get to go home early and they have four recesses. And they get to go home early. [*Scott reads. He comes to the section on "quiet time," when Amelia Bedelia makes her class read the stories out loud.*]

Martin, Rob, and Jed: "Quiet time."

Jed: No, it's loud time. Mrs. McLure, would you like it if we had loud time?

Pat [*laughing*]: I don't think I'll add that to our schedule.

Jed: Yesss.

Scott [*coming to part where they "practice the play"*]: Instead of their school play they go outside. See that's four, actually five recesses. And for math they get to go and steal apples. And they get to practice until the teacher's tired. Now that is—

Rob: They practice until they're tired?

Scott: No, the teacher. Now that is fun, fun, fun, fun.

In the end, Scott counts six recesses plus candy apples in class—the kind of day he would like to have.

Textual Realism

To this point, we have looked at children comparing text worlds to experienced worlds to determine the plausibility of stories. But they also test stories for internal coherence. A text can be unrealistic because parts of the narrative do not mesh. The narrative world itself may be a fantasy, but it must be internally logical. Scott was a particularly perceptive critic in the discussion of *The Stupids Die* (Allard and Marshall, 1981). At three points, he brought up what he saw as inconsistencies in the narrative or mismatches between the text and pictures. At one point, Buster, the Stupid boy, is eating with his feet, and the father says that he's finally learning table manners. Scott asked, "Then why aren't they [the parents] eating with their feet?" At the part about Buster mowing the carpet, Scott noted, "But it never grows back up again"—therefore Buster could only mow it once. When the Stupids eat in the shower and the father complains that his eggs are getting runny, Scott commented, "But it's impossible 'cause. . . . " And Rob and Jed finished the thought, with Jed observing, "He's not getting wet—just the kids and the mother, especially the mother." In each instance, Scott is not objecting to the silliness of the family (he loves that) but to what he sees as inconsistencies in the story.

The most complex example of this concern for textual consistency occurred in a sharing session in which Jimmy read Chris Van Allsburg's *The Polar Express* (1985). As he came to the picture where the elves are assembled to watch Santa give the first gift of Christmas, Phillip, an enthusiastic first grader, interrupted.

Phillip: Wow. That would be awesome to see that much elves. [*Jimmy continues reading. He mentions the "first gift of Christmas."*] What would I like for Christmas—every boy's toy in the world that I don't got.

After Jimmy finished the book, he asked for questions and comments, and there was a short discussion of other Chris Van Allsburg books. But Phillip had not forgotten his questions. Significantly, when adults read this book, they focus on the bell that Santa cuts for the narrator and the significance of his still being able to hear it as an adult. For Phillip, and I would guess for other children, the central interest comes earlier, when the boy can choose anything he wants for the first gift of Christmas—it is as if the narrator blew his opportunity by only asking for a bell. At any rate, Phillip comes back to his question.

Phillip: What would you want for Christmas if you were that boy?
Jimmy: I'm not sure.
Phillip: Do you got Nintendo?
Jimmy: No.
Phillip: If you wanted you could ask for that.
Jimmy: Anyway, this story is supposed to take place many years ago.
Pat: Why do you say that?
Jimmy: Well, because at the end of the book it says [*he reads*], "At one time most of my friends could hear but as the years passed it went silent for them. Even Sarah said on Christmas that she could no longer hear its sweet sound. Though I've grown old, the bell still rings for me as it does to all who truly believe."

76

Pat: I don't think I ever noticed about that part at the end. It does make it so that it's a story that happened years ago.

Jimmy: And there's no such thing as Nintendo all those years ago.

Pat: No, that's true.

Phillip: I think there was no such thing as TV.

Michelle: There was no such thing as electricity.

In this exchange, Phillip, who found Van Allsburg's story unrealistic (what boy would wish for a bell?), retold the story with himself as the asker. Jimmy noted that this retold narrative violated the internal logic of Van Allsburg's story because of problems with time. Phillip's wish would be inappropriate for the time frame of *The Polar Express.*

The discussion then shifted to the issue of electricity. The children noticed that there were no lights on the Christmas tree, and they tried to determine if that was because they were turned off—or because Michelle was right about electricity. Then the discussion shifted to toys, and Phillip came back to the wonderful opportunity that the boy in the story is given.

Phillip: I know what I would want if I was that boy.

Jimmy: What?

Phillip: A New Kids on the Block tape.

Jimmy: Hmmm. New Kids on the Block I don't think were even born then.

Phillip: I think they were maybe five or six years old then.

Abby: Then why would they be singing, Phillip?

Jimmy: They'd be as old as he would.

Phillip: Maybe little babies.

Jimmy seemed to juxtapose at least three time schemes in his responses to Phillip. First, there is the time when the story is told, by an older man looking back at his childhood. Second, there is the time when the story occurs, thirty or forty years before the time of the telling. And then there is nonstory time, the chronology of events occurring in the "real" world outside the story. Phillip wanted to see the boy in the story as a contemporary, as someone in his own position who could wish for Nintendo or a New Kids on the Block tape. Jimmy, on the other hand, realized that such a wish would violate the story time, in which the events occur much earlier. Matching up story time to "real time," he knew that Phillip's wish was unrealistic.

A friend of mine once called second grade the "adolescence of elementary school." Second graders seem transformed—poised, socially aware, concerned about dressing right, and anxious for those signs (e.g., pierced ears) of miniature adulthood. Their drawings are suddenly conventional: faces are "flesh colored" instead of the vivid greens or purples a first grader might choose. Friendship groups are more stable. They no longer explain their jokes. Along with this preadolescent adolescence comes a concern for what Jimmy called "the really real." The action of their worlds is suddenly bounded by physical and psychological principles. Jumping beans don't magically jump— and neither do people. From our vantage point as adults, we regret this new reluctance to accept magical explanations and label it a loss of innocence. But for children, I suspect, the inability to distinguish reality from fantasy is not always as charming as adults think it is. It makes for an unstable and shifting (and often frightening) world. I also suspect that, as the younger children in this class listened to Jimmy and Megan (and to the amazing Scott), they were attracted to this stabler, more rational world. The logic that demolishes Santa Claus and the Easter Bunny also makes the world a little less capricious.

There is a story about a mapmaker in fifteenth-century Genoa. A customer came in and asked to be shown a map of the world. "And where is the Roman Empire?" he asked. The mapmaker pointed.

"That small! And where is Genoa?"

The mapmaker pointed. "Just that dot."

"And where is this shop?"

"Oh, it is too small to even show."

"But doesn't that make you seem small and insignificant?" asked the customer.

"Well, not really. You see, I made the map."

We may be making the mistake of the customer if we insist on seeing this dismantling of a fantasy world as a loss to be mourned. From the standpoint of children, the new realism constrains the possible and helps them see the world as far more stable and open to understanding.

They are the mapmakers now.

78

6

Telling Stories

NEAR THE END of *The Catcher in the Rye*, Holden Caulfield reflects on an oral expression class he took at one of the several prep schools he had attended. In the class, students were coached to yell "Digression!" at any speaker who strayed from his topic. The "digression business" got on Holden's nerves because he liked it when someone digressed, it was "more *interesting* and all." He recalls a boy in the class who didn't stick to the point.

> There was this one boy, Richard Kinsella. He didn't stick to the point too much, and they were always yelling "Digression!" at him.... He made this speech about this farm his father bought in Vermont. They kept yelling "Digression!" at him the whole time he was making it, and the teacher, Mr. Vinson, gave him an *F* on it because he hadn't told what kind of animals and vegetables and stuff grew on the farm and all. What he did was, Richard Kinsella, he'd *start* telling you all about that stuff—then all of a sudden he'd start telling you about this letter his mother got from his uncle, and how his uncle got polio and all when he was forty-two years old, and how he wouldn't let anyone come to see him in the hospital because he didn't want anyone to see him with a brace on. It didn't have much to do with the farm—I admit it—but it was *nice*. (Salinger, 1951, 183–84)

Holden, unlike his former teacher, Mr. Vinson, views talk as organic, evolving, unpredictable. For him, it has the power to illuminate experience when it deviates from a preset agenda. He insists on the openness of talk, and, despite the urging of a battery of advisors that he reduce his life to a plan, he is unwilling to eliminate the role of chance in his life.

> A lot of people, especially this one psychoanalyst guy they have here, keeps asking me if I'm going to apply myself when I go back to school next September. It's a stupid question, in my opinion. I mean how do you know what you're going to do till you *do* it? The answer is, you don't. I *think* I am, but how do I know? I swear it's a stupid question. (213)

Vinson's class is a parody of normal classroom talk, but it doesn't miss the reality by much. Courtney Cazden (1988) argues that teacherly expectations for relevance and conciseness are often dramatically at odds with the storytelling patterns of students. She offers the following example in which a teacher seeks to narrow and focus a child's account of an outing. In her own way, the teacher is yelling "Digression!"

Nancy: I went to Old Ironsides at the ocean. [*Led by a series of teacher questions, Nancy explains that Old Ironsides is a boat and that it's old. The teacher offers the real name, the* Constitution. *Then Nancy tries to shift her story.*]

Nancy: We also spent our dollars and we went to another big shop.

T: Mm. 'N what did you learn about Old Ironsides? [*Led by teacher questions, Nancy supplies more information about the furnishings inside and the costumes of the guides, and then tries to shift focus again.*]

Nancy: And I had a hamburger, french fries, lettuce, and a—

T: OK. All right, what's—Arthur's been waiting and then Paula, OK? (16)

In a way, we can sympathize with the teacher's reluctance to allow the story to move to Nancy's lunch (and the rest of her outing). Arthur and Paula are waiting. But Cazden warns that "while there may be situational reasons for pressing children to speak relevantly and to the point, there are developmental and cultural reasons why it may be difficult for children to meet such expectations" (193).

Underlying this reluctance to allow stories and conversations to evolve is a concept of topicality or task-centeredness. Few distinctions in education are as uncritically invoked as those of on-task/off-task behavior or on-topic/off-topic talk. Most of the research I have read treats these binary distinctions as significant and self-evident. And if we think of the turn-of-the-century factory as the model for the classroom, it is easy to see why. Workers in these factories were typically involved in acting upon raw material in a preset way; they were not allowed to make decisions. Talk among themselves was considered a distraction, so breaks were instituted to segregate socializing from on-task work.

In reading, the student is the worker, the text the raw material, and understanding of the text is the uniform product the teachers (bosses) want manufactured. The primary action of the worker, aside from actually reading the text, is to answer questions about the text posed by the teacher or the collateral materials created by the reading system. Answering a question about the text is "on topic"; telling a story related to the text is "off topic." If a child tells a story, he or she is no longer working on the raw material of text to manufacture comprehension. The child has strayed from the assembly line.

According to this mechanical view of classroom talk, each text sets clear and firm boundaries for discussion—just as Richard Kinsella's topic, the farm, set boundaries for him. Yet one of the features of conversation is the shifting of topics: each turn shifts the topic to some degree; each speaker bridges to something new. Few social skills are as important as the capacity to handle what Irving Goffman has called "the etiquette of reach" (1976, 291). We admire the speaker who listens carefully and moves the discussion gracefully forward; we are put off by those who abandon topics that are still warm and cause the talk to lurch unpredictably. And I believe that we resist situations in which we cannot digress at all; we find it unpleasant to talk to people who must immediately get down to business, who resist any deviation, who always talk as if they are double-parked.

Goffman's term "etiquette of reach" is useful for looking at the storytelling that goes on in Pat's classroom. The word "etiquette" suggests that "topicality," being on topic, is socially defined instead of being a self-evident function of the texts under discussion. If we consider six- and seven-year-olds to constitute a culture, as I have argued, it becomes clear that the etiquettes of their social group may be quite different from those of adults (and even adult conversations, when they work, are less rigidly on topic than so-called discussions led by a teacher).

I became aware of these conventions several years ago when I was recording large group shares for a chapter in *More than Stories* (1989). It was chick season, and Joshua shared his three-page information book on chicks.

The eggs have to be turned twenty-two times and the last three days you do not turn them.

You must keep the incubator moist.

We put letters on one side, numbers on the other.

Imagine the questions you would ask regarding this text: Why do you keep the incubator moist? Why do you put letters on the side? The discussion turned out to be on copying machines. Pat asked how Joshua got the information on chicks.

Joshua: Well, we went to the library and we asked the librarian how we could get a copy of this paper and she said the copy machine and my mother said, "How does it work?" and somebody said, "I'll do it," and then they came over and they put the book like this [*demonstrates in pantomime*]. This was a heavy book. It had the picture like this and you put it like this and it goes "shhhhhhh" and then it spits out.

Aaron asked how long it took to learn the information, and Joshua answered, "One night." Then we were back to the copying machine.

Aaron: Did you mean when the copy machine spit out the paper did it go "vroo, vroo?"

Joshua: It just went "shhhhhh." The lady said it would spit out at you, but it didn't.

There were a couple of comments about Joshua's illustrations—and then back to copying machines.

Carin: Once when I went with Mrs. ———— we had to use the copy machine and she laid the book flat on the thing, whatever you call it. . . .

Joshua: They buckle it in, the book in. And it goes "shhhhhh" and then it comes out.

Carin: We just used Mrs. ————'s and we just put it flat down and then it just went "rrrrrr" like that and then she had to get it off and put another page on it until it was done.

As the discussion continued, several other students told their copying stories, each adding a new element, a new piece to the puzzle. John told about putting a cover over the book. Jimmy described a copier from his old school that was smaller and slower than the one Joshua used. Ginger told about working the copier at her dad's office and feeling the warmth of the copy as it came out.

In general, the members of Pat's class treated the text being shared, whether by a student or by a professional author, as a first long turn in a conversation. But a turn does not permanently fix in place the topic (or even the general theme) to be discussed. In the share group on Joshua's book on chicks, the ostensible topic of chicks was dropped once he told the more interesting narrative about using the copy machine. It was that narrative that set the theme for the discussion. According to the "etiquette of reach," this shift from chicks to copying machines was perfectly acceptable.

If the published text is treated as a turn in a conversation, it is no longer the inescapable focus of attention. It does not set fixed boundaries (patrolled by the teacher). Instead, it becomes one story among many. Ezra Jack Keats has his *Snowy Day,* and, as I watch the snow pile up on the frozen Oyster River, so do I. Keats takes his turn, and I take mine. His story evokes mine, enables me to see mine. The initiating text may become a focus for talk or, as in the case of Joshua's chick story, it may give way to a different kind of narrative, which in turn sets off a chain of stories. Ultimately, the stories go on forever. Ellen Blackburn Karelitz, who has described how this chain of narratives works in her own classroom, quotes one of her students, Brian: "You know, Mrs. Blackburn, when you said that numbers never end. Well, I just noticed something. Stories never end either" (1985, 13).

The Etiquette of Reach

According to Goffman, the etiquette of reach defines the kinds of bridges we can properly construct when taking a conversational turn. The speaker can "respond to something smaller or larger than the [previous] speaker's statement, or to one aspect of it, or even to the non-linguistic elements of the situation" (1976, 291). In the case of Joshua's sharing session, members of the class were not constrained to respond to the text being shared; they could pick up on a piece of

contextual information—using the copying machine—and then, as a
group, make that the central topic. This freedom to shift subjects, to
take an element from a previous turn and bridge to a new topic, was
the defining characteristic of their etiquette of reach. Sometimes the
shifts were so abrupt that Pat and I were left in the dust—along with
some of the second graders who played by more conventional rules.
In cases like these, Pat would not try to rein them in; she would ask,
"How is that connected? How did we get here?"

The purest example of this freedom to shift topics came in a
discussion of *The Night Before Christmas,* which Jennifer, a first
grader, shared. The experience of listening to this discussion was a
little like holding on to a runaway toboggan. Up to this point, the
group had talked about three Christmas shows, summarizing the
plots; they had noted the double-page illustrations in Jennifer's book;
and Pat had complimented Jennifer on her fluent reading. Then the
toboggan took off. As you read it, try to follow the bridges that
participants make to new topics. The ride begins with Jennifer
remembering other Christmas stories.

Jennifer: And that reminds me I got one that's about a reindeer.

Pat: Oh, another Christmas story.

Jennifer: And I got Christmas carols and my sister got Christmas
carols too. Kristy got *Santa's Runaway Elves* and Christmas
stories.

Pat: Um, you got lots of books.

Sandy: Well, I got *The Bear That Slept Through Christmas*—

Michelle: Me too.

Sandy:—and I got a pop-up book and a tape.

Jennifer: That reminds me. Last year I got Tic-Tacs. I don't remember
what else I got but I know I got some potatoes and oranges. I
didn't eat my oranges at all. It was all sort of plastic. So it
wasn't—

Sandy: What color Tic-Tacs did you get? Orange?

Jennifer: Light green.

Sandy: Light green? I like the orange.

Jennifer: So do I. I like the colored. Once my sister went to the
emergency room to get stitches. My mom was working and we

had to call my mom. Our neighbor is a nurse so she really needed to get stitches. She got seven stitches, two on top and five on bottom.

Michelle: I had four stitches all on my forehead.

Sandy: I've never had stitches.

Corrine: I've had stitches.

Michelle: They don't hurt at all. [*Overlapping talk about whether they hurt.*]

Pat [*to Jennifer*]: What made you remember that right now?

Jennifer: When she had green stitches.

Pat: Oh, she had green stitches and the green reminded you of Tic-Tacs.

Corrine: I had white stitches.

Michelle: When I first had my stitches it didn't hurt at all on my forehead.

Sandy: When you said stitches it reminded me of the day when . . . I think it was a wedding . . . and we went too and my aunts and my cousin and he was playing with the cat's toy and they had a glass table up there and it fell on the floor and he was on the couch on his knees and tried picking it up but he fell down and hit the glass and he had fifteen stitches.

Jennifer: That reminds me . . . that reminds me, my cousin's friend got a hundred stitches.

Corrine: Sandy reminds me of when I was a flower girl—

Sandy: I was too.

Corrine: My cousin, he was the person that carries the rings and he was looking over the balcony and he was at the hotel and he was looking over the balcony—and he didn't have the ring.

Pat [*laughs*]: You mean he lost the ring?

Corrine: But my aunt, she had one.

The conversation goes on for a couple more turns and concludes with Sandy saying to Pat, "Boy, that was a lot of talking." It surely was. Even Pat, with her considerable tolerance for digression, admitted that the discussion went "far afield" and wondered in the margins of the transcript whether she shouldn't have stepped in earlier. In four minutes, the conversation had shifted from *The Night Before Christmas* to Christmas books to Tic-Tacs to stitches to weddings.

Yet if we view the participants in this group as members of a six- and seven-year-old culture that has its own conversational rules, it is not as easy to dismiss such talk as off-topic and educationally insignificant. For one thing, members of the group easily found their way into the discussion, even Corrine, who was consistently reticent at other times. This ease of participation was created by the minimal bridge requirement. To take a turn, according to this requirement, a speaker must simply connect with any element in the previous turn, as when the greenness of Tic-Tacs led to a story featuring green stitches. The child may announce the connection with "that reminds me" but does not have to make the connection explicit.

This simple bridge requirement is less constraining than is the etiquette of other, more adult types of talk. One more stringent type of connection is the story-type bridge that we saw in the discussion of the copying machine. According to that constraint, a turn must connect to major thematic elements of the previous turn. For example, if someone tells a lost tooth story, the following speakers will also tell lost tooth stories (or stories that keep to major themes of that story type, such as pain, loss, or fear) until the topic becomes cold, at which point it is time for a more substantial shift.

An even more stringent rule might be called the text-based bridge. It is based on the presupposition that one text has priority in the discussion and that no bridge can take the speaker away from commentary on the text that has been given priority. Many conventional book discussions (and the report of Richard Kinsella) are expected to work within this more stringent set of constraints. Therapeutic and counseling discussions similarly focus on the principal narrative of the person seeking help.

From the standpoint of the six- and seven-year-old culture, however, the less stringent bridges seem the most congenial and allow for a wider range of participation. To exclude these less stringent bridges is to turn a deaf ear (literally) to this culture.

Stories and Community

Theories of reading comprehension have acknowledged the value of personal narratives, particularly *before* students read a text. By exploring and telling their prior knowledge, by activating frames of experience, readers put in place lenses that will help them comprehend a story. Rather than passively processing a story, they actively use this prior knowledge to anticipate what will happen. The story telling, according to this view, is subordinate to the act of comprehension, an oral means to a literate end.

In many of the book discussions in Pat's class, the priorities were reversed. The text activated schemas, suggested story types that enabled the children to tell their own stories. This is not to say there was no traditional comprehension work (for example, in the summaries). But it does mean that telling stories was not viewed simply as a means to comprehension. Pat does not continually nag students to get back to the text because the stories themselves are central to the way these groups work—just as they are central to all communities.

Collectively, the stories told by the group members celebrated life in rural New Hampshire. A great many concerned animals, wild and domesticated. Abby was the class expert on cats and had a seemingly inexhaustible set of stories about them. In one session, Jennifer asked Abby how her sister had named her cat. Abby responded:

> I don't know. Because her first name was Tiger Eyes because when her eyes closed up they looked like tiger eyes. And then she said, "Mom, I wish I could name her Jessica Fisher just like me" [*laughs*]. And my mom goes, "Go ahead, if you want to." And then she changed her name to Jessica Tiger Eyes Fisher. Probably by next year her name will be a different name.

Billy, as we have seen, loved tooth stories, but he also told dog stories.

> Once I saw this dog going past our house and then I saw three people running right after it. And then just when I opened the door to get out the dog came in our house and we had to get it out of the house. And then it went and people asked, "Did you see a dog coming into your house?" and we said, "Yes, it's over there." And they had to run all the way around and finally they caught it.

89

There was also a type of "gross" story that the boys told. The electricity scene in *Two Bad Ants* (Van Allsburg, 1988) reminded Martin of a dream.

> Last night I had a dream about this lady. She picked up the phone and then electricity started coming out and into her ear and she went "Ahhhhh." And the phone was being sucked into her ear and she kept on screaming and her body got all wrinkled and she fell down dead.

More typically, the gross stories involved the mutilation of insects like spiders:

Rob: My brother thinks that daddy longlegs have long legs so they take off and put them to make a web [*calls on Martin*].

Martin: That reminds me when we went to Scott's party, remember the part when we took the daddy longlegs spider and he picked off the legs and he saw the legs still moving.

Rob: Yeah.

Martin: That was neat.

Or flies:

Jake: Have you ever seen a black fly stick out his tongue?

Pat [*laughs*]: I don't think I've seen one.

Jake: That's what [the space creatures] look like. I've seen one. Really. They have this pink thing goes [*pantomimes it sticking out from his head*]. Because one day we were eating fish. We were camping and my dad caught some fish and we were eating it and all these flies came over and we had this fire and we started burning them up, all the flies. We would trap them and then sssssss [*sound of flies sizzling*].

While the mutilation stories were told only by boys, both sexes shared accounts of dealing with raccoons and skunks.

Susan: I think we had a raccoon in our house because our trash can was tipped over and there were four holes inside the trash can.

Sandy: That reminds me at my grandmother's house, one night. They're watching TV and then they heard a big bang out in the front and they went and they saw this mother raccoon and a baby raccoon. They knocked over the rubbish and they ran off.

Vicky: In "The Great Outdoors at Night" these raccoons get in a trash can and so in the morning the father has to clean up all the trash and the mother gets to cook.

Tommy: Just like a cat does.

Sandy: That reminds me once at my young Dad's friend's, well, a raccoon kept getting into the trash so he had to put these rocks on and one night they took a picture of a raccoon in someone else's chimney.

Each participant in the discussion added a new element to the general raccoon narrative (just as in the copier discussion). In Susan's, there was evidence of the raccoons' presence (teeth marks); in Sandy's first story, the raccoons are discovered, and the rubbish overturned; in Vicky's, the raccoons make a major mess; and, in Sandy's second story, the raccoon is photographed.

Many of these digressions during talk about animals could be justified fairly easily because they extended the children's knowledge of the natural world—reading time turned into science time. But the TV/video-game culture was also a major part of these children's experience, and it, too, made its way into the talk about books. For example, in the discussions of the *Stupids* books that I have quoted, the talk moved to TV shows and video games. The picture of the dog, Kitty, driving the car reminded Rob of a scene in "America's Funniest Home Videos."

Don [*pretending to be Kitty driving the car*]: RRRRRRRRRRR. There goes one door. RRRRRRRR. Konk. [*He makes an explosion sound to indicate a crash.*]

Jed: There goes everything.

Rob: On "The World's Funniest Home Videos" there was this person—

Jed: Oh, yeah.

Rob: He was in a car. There was only the front of it. But the back was broken off so there was only front wheels so he was like this [*demonstrates*] and driving the car.

Jed: Yeah, he was like this. The guy said, "Hey, Mom, do you like my new car?" And he was driving with the back off. And it worked good.

At another point in the discussion, the boys in the group made a fairly extensive inventory of video games. The picture of King Stupid the Fourteenth reminded Jed of the video game *King Friday the Thirteenth,* and they were off:

Jed: Have you ever played *King Friday the Thirteenth?*
Rob: King Friday the Thirteenth. Yeah.
Jed: It is fun.
Rob: Mm-hm.
Scott: How do you do it?
Jed: I don't know.
Don: It is a Nintendo game?
Jed: Yeah.
Scott: What do you do with it?
Jed: I don't know.

Don is reminded of the movie *Friday the Thirteenth.*

Don: I do not want to look at the cover of the movie *Friday the Thirteenth* one bit.
Pat [laughing]: No, I don't like it either.
Don: It's like URRRRRRRRR and it's like this gigantic thing bigger than the universe coming up and smashing the whole world into two thousand pieces.

Then the conversation goes back to how to play *King Friday the Thirteenth* and on to the games that Rob has rented—*Mario, Batman, Sesame Street,* and *Jeopardy.* Jed asks Rob how to play *Sesame Street,* and Rob starts a fairly complicated description of "Ernie's Magic Skates."

As I was transcribing this section of the tape, I inserted a question: "I would bet many teachers would try to get back to the book at this point. Why do you let them go on?" Pat's answer, I feel, was one of the most revealing comments she made concerning these groups.

> I'm not sure—I see this as a very interesting social situation for these boys. I feel almost like I'm eavesdropping on some "free play." It's like they're not really aware that we're there.

In reading and thinking about her answer, I realized that I was still thinking in binary terms—wondering when she would get back on task. But Pat does not view talk in on/off terms. She is interested in what children say and saw this talk about Nintendo games as important for the social functioning of this group. She didn't split the talk into social and academic, on task (what counts) and off task (what diverts). Her position is closer to one taken by Anne Dyson:

> Talk about academic tasks is often contrasted with social talk: individuals achieve because of the time they spend "on task." My observations suggest that the "academic" and the "social" are not so simply—or so profitably—separated. The social laughing, teasing, correcting, and chatting that accompany children's academic work are byproducts of the need to link with others and be recognized by them. But they can also be catalysts for intellectual growth. (1987, 417)

The share groups that failed were the ones that lacked social interaction and energy; they stuck to questions and answers (usually formulaic) about the book. They seemed to lack digressionary possibility. They never moved.

When Pat invites the children in her class to share their culture in reading groups, she subtly influences which parts of the culture they bring in. As I reread the video-game discussion, I was surprised to see that it really wasn't that long, not nearly as long as some lost-tooth discussions. I suspect that it seemed long because it was not the type of story—not the type of digression—that usually occurred. More typically, the stories featured animals, brothers and sisters, other books, topics that did not center on secondhand video experiences and on acquisitions.

A colleague of mine, Brenda Miller Power, who had spent considerable time in Pat's class once made the distinction between holiday time (measured by special days when children receive candy and presents) and seasonal time (ordered by natural growth and change). When Pat brings the brood hens into class, for example, she is announcing a preference for natural time. In this classroom, it is turning eggs, counting days, and then watching chicks hatch that mark the coming of spring. Likewise, stories of lost teeth and of younger brothers and sisters enable these students to measure their own growth.

Literature has the power to evoke these stories. It offers a way into memory. It opens up our own experiences and enables us to talk about them. Sometimes, when I see children tied to preset questions about a text, I imagine tiny lilliputian creatures dwarfed by the giant book that they are crawling over. The book is dominant and imposing; those attending to it are antlike to the point of insignificance. A more companionable image is of the author seated at a table—or better, with others around a campfire—ready to take the first turn in a conversation, to begin a chain of stories that cannot be predicted ahead of time. It's a position, I believe, that many authors would like to take.

7

"Get It?"

MY SON ANDY tells a joke.

"How did the monkey get out of the elephant's stomach?"

"I don't know. How?"

"It ran and ran until it got pooped out. Get it? Until it got pooped out. Out his butt. *Pooped out.*"

I got it the first time and considered it an improvement on his more typical jokes (Why did the chicken cross the road? It wanted to get breakfast). Andy thought his monkey joke was funny, not because of the play on words, but because it involved pooping. When his sister explained the play on words, he didn't think that added much to the humor.

Though poop jokes were not a regular feature of Pat's reading groups, humor and play with language were. The social importance of this humor can hardly be overstated; at times, laughter seemed to be the fuel that kept the kids going. And that laughter was kindled by the humorists that they read—Shel Silverstein, Harry Allard and James Marshall, Peggy Parish, Beverly Cleary, Marc Brown, Mike Thaler, Norman Bridwell, Stephen Kellogg, and many others.

What links this diverse group of writers is their common understanding of the wordplay and absurdity that characterizes first- and second-grade humor. For example, Beverly Cleary inserts one of the standard parodies of "Here Comes the Bride" into *Ramona Forever* (1985).

> Here comes the bride
> Fat, fair, and wide
> Here comes the groom
> Skinny as a broom
> Here comes the usher
> The old toilet flusher

Jimmy shared *Ramona Forever* three times, and each time, when asked the inevitable "favorite part" questions, he would sing this rhyme, often joined by someone else in the group. It was, after all, as close to toilet humor as they could safely get.

The advantages of joking and language play go beyond their obvious social value. Kieran Egan (1987) has claimed that "the beginnings of logic and philosophy . . . might involve encouraging each child to 'see' jokes and become jokesters" (468). He adds:

[A] capacity that tends to be very largely ignored in present curricula is the sense of humor. The early stimulation and development of the sense of humor, and even the sense of the absurd, seems to me to be ways of setting into place the foundations of logic and philosophy. Recognition of the categories deployed in arguing and thinking, and fluency in analyzing them, are integral to these disciplines. One of the areas in which fluency in analyzing categories occurs is the joke. (468)

For Andy's "pooped out" joke to work, it is necessary to take the expression both literally and figuratively (although for Andy, now, the literal is funny enough). Later metaphorical thinking will rely similarly on the capacity to fuse literal and figurative meanings.

To understand jokes like the one Andy told, children must move beyond the literalness that was common among the younger children in Pat's class. For example, in a discussion of *Tales of Oliver Pig* (Van Leeuwen, 1983), Pat asks why the author decided to write about pigs.

Adam: I think he liked pigs a lot. And it was dedicated for . . . it was "dedicated for David, the real Oliver Pig."
Pat: So you think that may have helped him.
Adam: Because . . .
Susan: Spit it out.
Adam: Oh, yeah, yeah, yeah. It meant that he wanted to do it because he liked pigs a lot and he wanted to do it for David.
Pat: Do you think David was a pig?
Phillip: Yeah.
Adam: Yeah, yeah, yeah, yeah.

David may be the "real Oliver Pig" but I suspect he wasn't a real pig. However, the tendency of the children was to take the literal meaning here.

We can see the same tendency in the following excerpt in which a group talks about the word "connections" (some groups ask for "comments, questions, or connections" when initiating book discussions).

Pat: Well, sometimes people do ask for connections, don't they? They say, "Comments, questions, or connections." Or sometimes "rememberings." Do you think connections are if you add something on in some way?

Jennifer: Yeah. 'Cause you connect them.

Pat: Because you connect them?

Jennifer: You connect a page on. You connect pages on.

Pat: Oh, I see.

Jennifer: Like you have to staple that thing to that thing.

Pat: Yeah. Yeah. That would make sense to use the word in that way.

Jennifer is clearly more comfortable thinking of the word *connection* in the more physical sense (attaching two things) than in the more figurative sense (recalling related personal stories).

This literalism can get in the way of understanding jokes, which often requires a split-second shift in one's frame of reference. We get the joke when we make that shift, when we see the second meaning that a word can have. Take, for example, the old Abbott and Costello routine: "Who's on first?" "Yeah, that's what I said, 'Who's on first?' " We get the joke when we understand that "Who" is both a player's name and an interrogative pronoun.

Even obeying routine requests requires us to distinguish among possible meanings of words, as Amelia Bedelia's troubles amply illustrate. These books (which seem tedious to me) bolster children's confidence that they can get a joke. In a way, Amelia's troubles are the same ones they have—recognizing that words have multiple meanings and determining which one is intended. When these books were shared in class, Pat pointed out a difference between the reactions of first and second graders: the second graders would laugh; the first graders would laugh—and then explain the joke. The younger children are just on the edge of "getting it" and feel a need to explain their reasoning.

Scott, in particular, was an explainer. Here is how he opened his session on *Merry Christmas, Amelia Bedelia* (Parish, 1987):

Scott: This book is about Amelia Bedelia and she doesn't understand things right like when it says "Pop six cups of corn" she pops six drinking glasses of corn, not the cups that you usually use. She just doesn't really understand things and when it says hang balls on the tree instead of bulbs she gets balls—baseballs, basketballs, bowling balls.

Martin: Where did it say she put a bowling ball on a tree? Where did it say bowling ball?

Scott: And it said trim the tree and she trims it. I never knew what it really means to trim the tree.

Pat: It means to decorate it.

Martin: She says that she thinks it's too bashful.

Scott: No. Maybe it's too fat. Maybe Mrs. Rogers thought it was a little too fat when they got it.

In a sharing session on *Arthur's Halloween* (Brown, 1982), Scott read the old joke about the graveyard being the most popular place because "people are just dying to get in." He stopped his reading and explained, "Not that kind of dying. Just like anxious to get in."

Abby, Michelle, and Billy also took their turns being explainers. In the sharing session on *Merry Christmas, Amelia Bedelia,* Scott came to the part where she is asked to "stuff the stockings" and she stuffs them as if she were stuffing a turkey.

Abby and Michelle: Uh-oh.

Michelle [*as if speaking directly to Amelia*]: Toys, not stuffing!

Scott: Stuff the stockings with toys?

Michelle: No, she's going to stuff it with stuffing.

Scott: I know.

Michelle: I hate that.

Earlier in the year, Abby shared *How Spider Saved Santa Bug,* by Robert Kraus (1989). At the end of the story, the reindeer have run away because of a fire and won't guide the sleigh. Spider saves the day by dipping a group of flies in glow-in-the-dark paint; the illuminated flies then guide the sleigh. Abby concluded, "And then Santa says something funny. He says, 'I hope the bedbugs don't bite.' And see, get it, they're bugs."

In a discussion of *Amelia Bedelia and the Baby* (Parish, 1982), Abby goes even further and explains the principle of double meanings.

> I think that when Amelia Bedelia does everything wrong she seems so dumb, like she doesn't know anything at all. There's two kinds of a thing, and she does the other thing and not the thing that she's supposed to. She doesn't know the difference between them.

Children can look at Amelia Bedelia as they sometimes look at their less mature younger brothers and sisters.

Billy's talk was full of plays on words and with words, some of which were so elaborate that they were hard to follow. In a discussion of *Ira Sleeps Over* (Waber, 1972), he read a phone conversation that begins with "What are you doing?" where the response is "Talking to you." (Michelle responds, "Get it? 'Talking to you.' ") This reminds Billy of a conversation he had with his mother.

> I once had this book about [*inaudible*] and one time I said to my mom, "Read this book."
> And she said, "What's this book?"
> "It's a book."
> And my mom said, "What's a book?"
> And I said, "A book."
> And then my mom said, "Read it."
> I said, "Read the cover of the book."
> And my mom, she read the book but forgot to read the cover of the book. So I heard the book but I didn't hear what it was.

When I first heard this story I thought Billy was just being silly. But as I reread it, it appeared that Billy was playing with the meaning of *book*. Is a book the title of the book? We do use the word that way—"My favorite book is *Huckleberry Finn.*" Or is the book the actual text? His mom read him the book without reading the cover; she read the book without reading the book.

Billy played with the idea of throwing your voice in a discussion of *Phil the Ventriloquist* (Kraus, 1989). In the book, Phillip, a bunny, throws his voice and scares away a robber. The secret to throwing your voice, according to Phillip, is eating carrots.

Vicky: If I eat a lot of carrots I hope I can throw my voice [*she laughs*].

Billy: I do eat carrots every night.

Vicky: Billy.

Billy: I have two. It's kind of dangerous to throw your voice—you might lose it.

Vicky: Yeah.

Billy: And also if you throw your voice and then you forget where it is then you kind of like [*mimics mouthing words without being able to speak*]. If a friend says, "How are you?" and you go [*pretends to be unable to speak*]. I mean, really.

Not surprisingly, Billy was attuned to plays on words in the books being shared. In Steven Kellogg's version of the Chicken Little fairy tale, a Sky Patrol helicopter crashes near the end. In the wreckage, we can see only the word *Sky* on the door—leading everyone to conclude that the sky indeed has fallen.

Billy: It was funny when it dropped out of the sky.

Michelle: The acorn falling?

Billy: Right here [*points to book*]. It says "Sky." The sky is falling. See the "Sky"?

Michelle: See. I get it now. See, the helicopter is from the sky so he thinks the helicopter just went in there. And he thinks the sky is falling.

Michelle worked hard to get it, but, unlike Billy the linguist, she was not focused as specifically on the language game. She seemed to be arguing that because the helicopter is from the sky, its falling is a clue that the sky is falling, too—which is pretty fair reasoning in itself.

The child who cannot pick up multiple meanings is excluded from full participation in a culture—like Amelia Bedelia herself. All of us who have tried to learn another language can attest to the problem both of acquiring foreign idioms and of directly translating our own. Even among English-speaking peoples, the multiple meanings of expressions can cause problems, as they did for a female British teacher who came to this country and invited a man she had just met to "knock [her] up some time."

Getting it is important for more than deciphering jokes. If the language we use is open to multiple meanings, our social competence depends on our ability to figure out the one intended. Without that capacity, children have weaker understanding of human intentions. For example, in *The Teacher from the Black Lagoon* (Thaler, 1989), a little boy hears from an older brother that Mrs. Green, his teacher, is "a real monster," and he imagines this real monster as a cross between an alligator and a dragon (who in his dream incinerates one of the class members). The boy's terror comes from his literalness. He is not yet able to understand that when we use the word *real* in this way, we usually intend something quite different from the literal meaning: that Mrs. Green is *like* a monster; that Oliver is *like* a pig. The child who can make these distinctions is on surer social footing.

Absurdity

A Day with Wilbur Robinson (Joyce, 1990) centers around a hunt for the false teeth of Wilbur's grandfather, who cannot look for them himself because he is busy in his lab, teaching frogs the big band sound with the help of Duke Ellington and Louis Armstrong. At dinner time (with the teeth still not located), the young narrator sits with Wilbur's family at the dinner table. Uncle Gaston shoots meatballs out of a small cannon toward the open mouths of Grandfather Robinson and Uncle Judlow, who is still wearing his brain augmentor, a helmet with about twenty electric wires running out from it. At the center of the table, a frog entertains. Two birds, wearing fezes, sit across from the narrator next to cousin Pete and his pet tiger. The meal is being served by an octopus named Lefty (get it—an octopus named Lefty).

Some of the most popular books in Pat's class (for the boys, clearly *the* most popular ones) had this bold, extravagant humor. Billy's favorite was *Cloudy with a Chance of Meatballs* (Barrett, 1978), which he mimicked in his writing. Rob, Martin, and Jed went through a *Stupids* phase. Jake's favorite was *Company's Coming* (Yorinks, 1988), which featured aliens looking like giant insects who visit a family. ("We come in peace. Do you have a bathroom?") The military is alerted and brings an arsenal to destroy the package the aliens have brought—which turns out to be a blender. These and more.

The absurdity of this humor fits well with the humor of the boys. In Patricia Reilly Giff's *Snaggle Doodle* (1985), the characters must make an invention out of a balloon, a cereal box, a belt, some socks, and a flashlight.

Pat: What do they make of all that?
Corrine: Do they make the inventions?
Cindy: Well, they just put the parts together and they make an invention.
Tommy: A smelling machine—to smell the socks.
Pat [laughing]: A machine to smell socks?

There is a play on family names in Beverly Cleary's *Ramona Forever* (1985), with the Quimby family experimenting with Philbert and Abelard as possible first names for the new baby.

Allan: Well, my mom told me that when we were naming Billy, I wanted to name him Flag.
Pat: Flag?
Jimmy: Flag? Allan, did you really want to name your brother Flag?
Allan: I did.
Jimmy: Very weird.

They enjoyed the absurdity of the prizes in Steven Kellogg's *Can I Keep Him* (1971):

Martin: Well, the boy won a python and the second prize was a trip to the moon, and third prize was six fat grapefruits, and fourth prize was only a raisin.
Vicky [laughing]: He's having one raisin.

And this theme of rewards figured into a story Martin told about the first time he ever put something under his pillow. He received a quarter—for a fingernail.

As might be expected, no one enjoyed the absurd more than Billy. In my music room interview, I asked for expected questions, and the group dutifully supplied them.

Michelle: "Why did you decide to read that book?"
Megan: "Is that your reading book?"
Billy: And "Are you alive?"
Newkirk: "Are you alive?"?
Jimmy: If you're talking I guess you'd have to be alive.

When he shared *The Little Fish That Got Away* (Cook, 1956), Billy singled out the line about the boy "never catch[ing] anything except a cold"—which drew laughs from the group. This line echoed his own sense of humor. One day before snack, Pat said to the group, "Satisfy your hunger." Billy replied that he wasn't hungry.

Pat: You're not hungry? You had a good breakfast?
Billy: No, I didn't have any.
Pat: You didn't have any breakfast?
Billy: No.
Pat [*skeptically*]: Billy.
Billy: I had air for breakfast.

Some of my favorite exchanges occurred when Billy, the games player, was teamed up with Jimmy, the class realist. Billy would sometimes play off the more adult language that Jimmy used in the group. After recess one day, Jimmy began to resummarize *Ramona Forever,* and Martin balked.

Martin: You told us at the beginning.
Jimmy: I know but I just want to refresh everybody's memory.
Billy: My memory's already fresh. I don't have one, remember.
Jimmy: I think everybody should calm down.

Among the girls, Vicky seemed to bring the same sense of play to the groups. In a discussion of dogs, Susan was searching for the name of her favorite breed.

Susan: I know what it looks like but I forgot the name of it. And it comes in different colors.

Vicky: Even purple and pink.

Susan: It comes in different colors like brown or white or sometimes it even comes in reddish.

Pat's comment: "Susan's not going to play."

Another ritualized form of absurdity was the game of progressive exaggeration, which even Jimmy would try on occasion. In my interview with Billy, Megan, Jimmy, and Michelle, there were two examples of this one-upmanship. I asked the groups how they picked books, and Megan patiently explained.

Megan: Like I should pick a larger book. I shouldn't pick one of those little orange books. I could read that in a minute.

Billy: I could read it in a second.

Later in the interview, Jimmy complained about how many times he has heard *Arthur's Halloween* (Brown, 1982) and inadvertently prompted another competition.

Jimmy: I've read every single Arthur book, and I've read *Arthur's Halloween* five times.

Michelle: I've read *Arthur's Halloween* six times.

Billy: I've read *Arthur's Halloween* ten times.

Michelle: Yeah, right, Billy.

Even when he was not competing, Billy enjoyed exaggerating the truth, as he did in a discussion of *The Mystery of the Missing Red Mitten* (Kellogg, 1974). Pat asked Billy if he had ever lost his mittens, and Billy said no, but he *had* lost "three horses and nineteen pairs of kittens."

During a discussion of Ezra Jack Keats's *The Trip* (1987), even Jimmy took part in an exaggeration game. Pat had encouraged Megan to bring in some shoebox art and suggested that maybe others in the class would bring in shoeboxes.

Vicky: I have a hundred shoeboxes.

Pat: Do you?

Jimmy: I have a thousand.

Sandy: I have about ten thousand.

Abby: I use all of mine for present boxes.

Jimmy: I have at least a million.

This time, it was Megan who brought the talk back to what was really real.

Sound Games

In Jan Stepian's book *The Hungry Thing* (1988), a large animal (that looks a little like Bigfoot) walks into town carrying a sign that says "Feed Me." The townspeople wonder aloud what they should feed the Hungry Thing, who responds with words like "schmancakes" and "tickles." The wise men get it all wrong. They think that tickles are "curly tailed hot dogs that grow in a row." A little boy is the only one who can understand what the Hungry Thing is saying. "Schman-cakes" *sounds like* "pancakes"; "tickles" *sounds like* "pickles." The Hungry Thing is finally fed and turns his sign around; it now reads "Thank you."

The story, like "The Emperor's New Clothes," is a variant on the classic folktale in which a child's perception is superior to that of adults. The wise men in *The Hungry Thing* make the serious mistake of not attending to the sounds of the words, thereby missing the critical clue. The boy worked on a chain of sound similarities to arrive at the Hungry Thing's intended meaning. As I reviewed the transcripts, I thought that this story also might be read as a parable or an inverted story of human development. Typically, the developmental narrative is one of progress, from lower to higher levels of reasoning (the metaphor of height is typically invoked). Yet, in *The Hungry Thing,* the child is the superior problem solver because he still can hear the language of the wild thing as *sound.*

In precisely the same way, the younger children in the share groups could hear and play with the sounds of words that I no longer heard. They would celebrate rhymes by repeating them, as if they didn't want to let go of them. "Uh-oh spaghettios" became a standard response to any impending trouble. When they were reading *Arthur's Halloween* (Brown, 1982), they would always turn to the epitaphs on the tombstones, particularly this one:

Scott: "Here lies the body of Sally Bent. She kicked up her heels and away she went."

Jed: "And away she went" AHHHHHHHH [*leans back on the chair as if falling*].

Jimmy: I guess she's a skeleton now.

Jed [*to himself*]: "She kicked up her heels and away she went."

In the discussion of *The Hungry Thing,* Pat asked Adam to extend the story.

Pat: Did you think of any other foods you might add to that—

Adam: I'd add peas.

Pat: What would you call them?

Adam: Glees. [*Pat laughs.*]

On another day Adam recited the Shel Silverstein poem "Gumeye Ball" (1981, 68), which, according to Pat, "appeals to some of the boys who want a touch of the gross in their poetry."

Phillip also enjoyed these spontaneous rhyming games. In one discussion, Megan was talking about her own poetry writing.

Megan: I did one about a brontosaurus.

Pat: What did you rhyme with brontosaurus?

Megan: I didn't rhyme that one.

Phillip: Hauntasaurus.

Megan: Hauntasaurus.

Phillip: Contasaurus, too.

Had Billy, Michelle, or Vicky been in the group, my guess is this game could have gone on for a while—but it isn't one that Megan, a second grader, wanted to play.

No one enjoyed the sounds of words more than Vicky; she would pick up on words she liked and repeat them, as she did in one discussion of Beverly Cleary's *Ramona Forever.* Allan noted that one of the chapters is called "It."

Pat: The chapter is just called "It"? Do you have any idea what that might be about?

Allan: Up on the top it says, "It" and that's a chapter.
Vicky: And the whole world should say, "It, it, it, it, it, it, it, it, it."

In another session, Vicky was asked about something that appears to be writing in one of the pictures.

Vicky: See, he just had a little scribble scrabble.
Pat: So you don't really know what his name is. They didn't even use
  real tiny letters here.
Vicky: Right, they just used scribble scrabble.

A couple of turns later, Tommy said, "I guess his name is Scribble Scrabble." For both Vicky and Tommy, the pleasure of this exchange was not trying to figure out what the name on the tree is—but in saying the words "scribble scrabble."

Even Melanie, generally reluctant to participate because of her late entry into the class, began to play the sound game. In one of the share sessions, Pat noted that all of the children's names began with M.

Michael: First me, then Martin, then Michelle, then Melanie.
Pat: This is the M group today.
Melanie: Ooh. The M group. It's M M M M M M M MMMMMM-
  MMMMM.

Pat noted: "I'm glad to see her playing with sounds and letters. It's what so many of the others have done but she didn't until recently. An indication of her comfort and awareness of words and sounds."

Another version of wordplay is very similar to that performed by the boy in *The Hungry Thing*. A reference to Peewee Scouts in one book immediately reminded others in the group of Pee-wee Herman. A reference to Captain Cook reminded Michelle of Captain Hook. In one curious session, Abby's story of dolls suddenly changed to a discussion of money and bank deposits. As we looked at the transcript, it became clear that the shift was from "dolls" to "dollars." In another conversation that occurred before a session began, the children played with the word "friction."

Sandy: Jake, I got a friction rod.

Jed: A fraction rod.

Jake: A friction rod. A fiction rod.

Jed: A fiction rod. It tells stories.

For me, and I would guess for many adults, these possibilities for association of sound recede as we become older. Like the adults in *The Polar Express,* we lose the capacity to hear the bell—to hear the words—as we grow older. Language, even oral language, is all semantics, no phonology. A loss.

It was near the end of a long sharing session, and Billy was particularly restless. He was one of those boys who was always restless—his major complaint about reading groups was that Pat required them all to sit in their chairs and not stand leaning on the table. (Billy admitted he faked sitting most of the time.) Billy was getting goofy.

Billy: And if I read it backwards, this is what it sounds like: "Snowman the of heart the was mitten my heart a with snowman a chest his on spot that what melting is snowman . . . "

Pat [*laughing*]: What made you want to do that?

Billy: It sounds funny.

Pat: It does. It doesn't make much sense.

Billy's demonstration interested Megan, who entered the discussion.

Megan: What if someone read a book like that by accident? They didn't know how to read a book and they just read it backwards.

Pat: Do you think that's why they put on the books they were writing "Open this side"?

Billy [*after continuing to read backward*]: Megan.

Megan: I think it would sound even funnier if you read the words backwards, too. That would make more sense because you're reading it backwards but you're reading it forwards, too.

Billy: "The Mystery of the Missing . . . " [*tries to read mitten backward and laughs*].

There is something paradoxical, riddlelike, in Megan's response to Billy's demonstration. It might be formally stated: "How can you read forward and backward at the same time?" The conundrum in Billy's earlier story about his mother's reading to him could be stated: "How can you read a book without reading the book?" The riddle, like the joke, like the play on words, demands that we not be tied to the fixed conventional meaning of words. If we think of *book* as a conventional, unambiguous concept, we miss Billy's joke. If we think of moving backward and moving forward as mutually exclusive, we can't solve Megan's riddle.

This may be silliness—but it is silliness of a very high order.

8

The Enigma
of Instinct

MY BROTHER, WHO for a year played varsity basketball at Harvard, once told me why he never made the starting lineup. The players on the second team were as big as the starters, as fast, and they seemed to run the plays with greater precision. If my brother was supposed to take a shot from the top of the key, that's where he took it. It was the way he had been taught in high school—to carry out the plays as diagrammed. This discipline, we had all been told, would prepare us for The Game of Life (how many times did we hear that expression at sports banquets?). In our town it was generally agreed that Life modeled itself after the National Basketball Association.

The play of the starters seemed less careful than that of the reserves. Shots were not taken from the diagrammed spots. Plays were altered in midexecution. A player with a "hot hand" might shoot before a play had a chance to develop. At first, this unpredictable style of play looked to my brother like chaos, a violation of the code of performance instilled in him by his coaches in high school. But as he watched (and he had plenty of time to watch), he began to see the difference between the outer game and the inner game. He excelled at the outer game, which was played to a specified set of rules. But the inner game was not as random or chaotic as it first appeared; it was guided by a subtle and shifting reaction to context. The skilled players of the inner game reacted to the flow of the game, creatively modifying or rejecting the playbook. The game itself suggested possibilities to them. It is the same phenomenon that writers describe when they talk about "listening" to the evolving writing.

To claim, as I will, that the act of teaching is composed of an inner and outer game is a sign, I suppose, of the incurable male addiction to sports metaphors. Too many banquets. But the distinction is useful. As in sports, it is possible to describe procedures for setting up groups, ways of helping students choose books, methods for record keeping, procedures for evaluation. This outer game can be diagrammed, specified in curriculum manuals and methods textbooks. And this information is clearly useful. Nevertheless, it provides little insight into the moment-by-moment decision making of the skilled teacher. It does not account for the particularity of individual situations, individual students. Beginning teachers regularly complain that college methods courses are inadequate because they don't (and probably can't) teach them this inner game.

115

The problem sensed by these beginning teachers is obvious. The inner game is difficult to explain. For many skillful teachers, it is tacit, intuitive, seemingly instinctual. When I first asked Pat why she switched over to her reading-process approach, her first response was, "It felt right." And in the act of teaching, so many decisions are made with such speed that there is no time for deliberation. David Schon writes:

> When we go about the spontaneous, intuitive performance of the actions of everyday life, we show ourselves to be knowledgeable in a special way. When we try to describe it we find ourselves at a loss, or we produce descriptions that are obviously inappropriate. Our knowing is ordinarily tacit, implicit in our pattern of actions and our feel for the stuff with which we are dealing. It seems right to say our knowing is *in* our action. (1983, 49)

Schon is arguing against the traditional model of knowing, where practice is viewed as the application of theoretical knowledge produced by an expert class. Instead, he claims, there is a kind of knowing that does not come from a prior intellectual operation or the application of an abstract preexisting theory. The tightrope walker's know-how lies in, and is revealed in, the way she takes her trip across the wire.

Even for those of us who spend time in her classroom, Pat's style is elusive, difficult to articulate as a set of principles. In an interview with her, I asked if she had a strategy for participating in the groups. She answered:

> Not necessarily. That's almost an instinctive sort of thing. It's usually either because something really interesting has come up and I want to take part in the discussion. Sometimes because I think that maybe by coming in I can instigate a little more discussion from others—but I'd rather hold back and see what they're doing first. If you don't start with your own agenda, and let the groups take over, then you can react to it rather than being the one who controls it.

When I began tape-recording, one of my goals was to understand the instinctiveness of her decisions. But this instinctive type of knowing, what Michael Polanyi has called "tacit knowing," often seems to defy definition. According to Michael Carter, "experts react intuitively to most situations, relying not on rules or plans or strategies, but on the familiarity that comes with experience" (1990, 272).

I slowly began to realize that the information I was looking for could not be reduced to general statements of principle or philosophy. This skill is contextual, personal, particular, local; it can be revealed but not abstractly defined.

Studies of expertise, particularly studies of master chess players (a favorite subject of cognitive researchers), support the importance of local knowledge in skilled behavior. Initially, it was thought that expert chess players had better memories than novices, yet when pieces were randomly placed on the board, no difference was found. However, when the pieces were placed in meaningful places (positions that they might actually assume in a game), the masters could remember them far more accurately than novices could. Researchers estimate that Grand Master chess players can recognize about fifty thousand meaningful chess configurations; they can play effectively because of their rapid recognition of these playing situations.

There is, to be sure, a considerable difference between moving wooden chess pieces and dealing with live and lively children in a classroom. But some of the skill of experienced teachers is very likely due to a capacity—refined by experience—to identify individual situations carefully and then to react accordingly. Where an outsider might consider a boy to be misbehaving according to the crude template that defines disruptive behavior, an experienced teacher can probably read the situation far more precisely (e.g., "he is acting out to avoid work that he is unsure he can do—like his older brother at this age."). Just as the chess master can see more meaningful positions, the experienced teacher carries a rich collection of lenses for assessing student work and behavior. What separates the experienced teacher from the novice is not generalized theory but a refined, particularized capacity to read situations.

This is not to say that experienced teachers do not act upon theories (although some academicians often accuse them of this crime). Rather, our theories, the ones that guide the literally hundreds of decisions we make each day, are not abstract in the same way that scholarly theory is. A teacher's theories often take the form of scenarios of situations they have seen before and possible ways of dealing with them (analogous to the chess master's knowledge of chess positions). The theory, if it is articulated at all, is embedded in stories about individual students—"Yeah, I had a kid like that last year, each day I had to. . . . " Stephen North (1987, 23–27) has called this type of knowledge "lore"—it is oral, storylike, personal, and not subject to validation by a higher authority (i.e., a researcher). Collectively, these scenarios, these microtheories, provide a precise guide to decision making that conventional theories cannot possibly match.

While it is difficult, if not impossible, to articulate these very specific theories in response to the blunderbuss question that I initially asked, they can be discussed in reference to specific exchanges. Take, for example, Pat's commentary on this section of Jennifer's share session on *How Spider Saved Easter* (Kraus, 1988).

Jennifer: It's about Spider and Fly and I think it's Ladybug. She wants to win first prize. She gave out the Easter baskets that she was going to leave but the chocolate bunnies melted so then she wanted to win first prize in a fair contest. And the spider—
Pat: What's the contest?
Jennifer: The contest is . . . I don't know if they put that in the book.
Allan: For the best hat.
Jennifer: It's a contest for the best hat.
Pat: So it's a contest for the best Easter hat?
Jennifer: Yeah.

Pat entered into this exchange much earlier than she usually does—in fact, before Jennifer had even finished her summary. In her commentary, Pat wrote:

> Jennifer sometimes needs a little help with comprehension. She concentrates so much on word reading she can lose the idea. In this case I had a clue that she didn't understand from her written book response.

Pat's intervention was based on her understanding of how Jennifer tended to read and on the evidence of her summary and her previous written work on this book. Pat's commentary reveals that she was working from a situation-specific, student-specific theory.

In this chapter, I will draw on Pat's commentaries to try to show her "knowing in action" as she assumes various roles in the sharing groups. At the same time, however, I acknowledge that no description can adequately explain a teacher's instinctiveness; I cannot begin to account for the literally thousands of decisions Pat made while she participated in the groups I recorded. My purpose resembles more that of the ancient cartographers when they marked off the unknown territory on their maps. I will start with a broad definition of the various roles Pat took and quote from transcripts and commentary to show how she worked in each one.

Organizing and Keeping Time

Despite the open, sometimes unpredictable nature of the sharing groups in Pat's class, some things are not open to alteration. The general order of a turn (naming the book, summarizing, asking for questions and comments) is standard. And every child in each share group receives a full turn, even if that means the sharing group gets back together at 10:30 after recess. To keep things on schedule (even a loose one) requires Pat to act as stage manager, particularly in the early weeks, when children are not familiar with the routines. She will remind them of the procedure, as in this exchange with Vicky.

Vicky: *The Fire Cat* by Esther Averill [1960]. That's "Pickles," my favorite word.

Pat: And your book, like Allan's book, is going to be too long for us to hear the whole book. So do you want to think about just how much you're going to share with us and what you're going to tell us?

The two most difficult parts of the procedure for the first graders are selecting a part of a book to share and dividing a presentation into a summary and a reading (as we've seen, they preferred to jump right into reading). Here is how one of Jennifer's early turns began.

Jennifer: Ready. *Go Dog Go* by P. D. Eastman [1961].
Pat: I like the way you told us the author right away.

Jennifer [*reading first page and then stopping*]: I like the part when they go up the tree and they have a funny hat on [*continues reading*].

Pat: Do you want to skip to the part that you'd like to share?

Of course, Jennifer wanted to share the whole thing.

One of the advantages of the multigrade classroom is that Pat can rely on the second graders to help the younger children with the routines.

Pat: Remember what we talked about a little bit last week about sharing groups? What are some of the things that people should do in sharing groups? Megan.

Megan: Well, they talk about the book a little bit.

Pat: Why is it helpful for us to have somebody talk about it for a little bit?

Megan: Because if someone else wants to have it then you wouldn't have to read the whole book. They would be able to remember what the book is about.

Pat noted, "Megan's a great one to have in the group. She understands about summaries and 'setting the stage' for oral reading."

Supporting Student Talk

A few years ago, I spoke with a researcher who was studying what is called "back-channel" talk, the "mm-hms" with which we punctuate what others say to us. Within minutes, I became aware of every time I said "mm-hm," and the conversation quickly became an awkward comedy routine.

"I'm studying the places where people use 'mm-hm.' "

"Mm-hm. Oh God, there I said it again."

For a while, I tried to suppress the "mm-hms," but like a twitch, they reappeared.

However unglamorous (barely above a grunt), back-channel talk is crucial for the speaker. Few things are more unnerving than to speak to someone who does not support us with these verbal cues that indicate attention and encourage us to go on. The "mm-hms" suggest to the speaker that the listener recognizes the turn is not over, that he or she is not impatient to take a turn. They seem to say, "Keep going; take your time. Even make another attempt at what you're trying to say. I'm still with you." They provide a critical split second for the speaker to reload, to think ahead. I'm reminded of how much I need this support every time I stutter a message into an answering machine.

The "mm-hm" is one of many ways in which Pat supports student talk. For example, it allowed Billy to extend a fishing story. Pat had asked Billy if his rod and line were like those of the boy in *The Little Fish That Got Away* (Cook, 1956).

Billy: No, I didn't have wood and I didn't have a pin. I had a hook. It was very sharp.

Pat: Mm-hm.

Billy: You see but if you have a bobber you just have a little pole. You just take a little pole. You don't [*demonstrates pulling up abruptly on rod*] or you might hurt the fish too much and it might be a teeny one. Just go [*demonstrates casting*] and then you can wind him in or go slowly slowly back.

Pat: Mm-hm.

While I couldn't read Billy's mind, it did seem at least possible that Pat's first "mm-hm" gave him both encouragement and time to formulate his comments on reeling in fish. The language itself changed at that point, from a listing of differences to a more complex (and not totally clear) contrast between fishing with a pole and fishing with a rod and reel. And even after Billy finished the contrast, Pat came in with a second "mm-hm," offering him more time to talk on the topic.

When I was transcribing, these "mm-hms" were so common (and, to be honest, so uninteresting), that I'm sure I missed a great many of them—they became almost background noise. But this regular undramatic reassurance surely plays a major role in sustaining students through long or complex utterances.

Another form of support is to repeat what the children have said in such a way that they are invited to continue the thought. The following short exchange is very typical.

121

Megan: I want to share some of my scary ones [i.e., poems].

Pat: Scary ones?

Megan: Yeah. I have one about all Halloween things, one about spiders, one about witches, one about ghosts. I like the ghost one best.

Although I have punctuated Pat's response as a question, it is really more an invitation to expand—" 'Scary ones'? Tell me more about them." We can see the same invitation to continue in this excerpt from a discussion in which Michelle shared a book on chicks.

Pat: So what things did it tell you in there that you've seen chicks doing?

Michelle: Well, when we had the incubator I saw a baby chick hatch.

Pat: You saw it hatch like that one.

Michelle: Uh-huh. But it didn't. And it popped out like that. But it wasn't fuzzy. It was just like wet and it wanted to take a nap just like that.

In an interview, Pat commented on this strategy.

> I do a lot of repeating, or in a way clarifying what they said, saying it back to them as the way I understood it. That kind of validates for them what they've said. It gives it value. Sometimes by repeating it I highlight it a bit more. And sometimes it helps to make more sense of the comment for everybody. They know what you've understood from what they've said and they can go beyond that.

As I've shown, one strategy is simply to repeat with a slight questioning inflection. The student then picks up with a "yeah" and continues with the turn. There are at least two variations on this repeating strategy. In one, Pat repeats the comment and then asks a question.

Pat [asking about The Z Was Zapped (*Van Allsburg, 1987*)]: Which one surprised you most? Which was the most unusual?

Jed: The Z.

Jennifer: I would say the Y.
Pat: You thought the Y. What was happening to the Y?

Another example of the repeat-and-question strategy occurred in a discussion of *The Blue Ribbon Puppies* (C. Johnson, 1958).

Adam: What's your favorite pup?
Vicky: The spotty one.
Pat: The spotty one? Why do you like the spotty one?
Vicky: He just looks cute with all the spots on him.

We can see the same pattern in a discussion of lost mittens that took place after Billy shared *The Mystery of the Missing Red Mitten* (Kellogg, 1974).

Pat: Have you lost mittens before?
Billy: Yeah, but I found them.
Pat: You did find them? You've always been able to find them when you lost them?
Billy: Yeah.

In the other repeating strategy, Pat rephrases a student's answer in a way that clarifies it. In this excerpt of a discussion about *Arthur's Valentine* (Brown, 1985), Pat restates the reason that Sandy gives for her theory about Arthur's motivation.

Pat: Do you think that Arthur was real upset with Francine?
Sandy: Well, he might have been because she invites him to the movies and he sat in row three A. It says, "Francine smiled at Arthur. 'So you're my secret admirer,' said Arthur. 'Yes, four eyes.'" That's when he went to sit down. And I think he was a little mad because his arms were crossed.
Pat: Oh, is that the way someone would sit if they were angry?
Sandy: My sister sits like that when she is angry with me.

These ways of responding are clearly not revolutionary innovations, as Pat would be the first to admit. They are basic ways of

123

attending to a friend, a student, a guest; they provide psychological space to extend an initial comment, to keep the floor. Individually, they look minor indeed. But cumulatively, they are integral to developing an environment where students hold the floor. And they require the sustained attention of the teacher; you cannot repeat a comment that you haven't heard.

Shifting the Conversation

Typically, in book discussions, any observation not directly related to the content of the reading is considered off topic. As should be apparent by now, Pat takes a much more expansive view of the range of appropriate comment.

> They get away from the book. Yet in many ways it is the book that has triggered some thought in their mind or helped them remember some experience. It's all part of putting that reading into a context for them. So just because they're not answering specific questions directed at the passage, I think it's still valuable for them. I think there's so much they can learn by exploring their thoughts and being able to go far afield and then pull it back in. They learn about discussions. They learn about the relevance of different topics. They learn from each other, and they learn about each other.

I'm sure that one reservation that teachers might have about the approach as I've presented it thus far is that, if the text serves merely to trigger associated memories, students may spend too little time actually commenting on it. If the text is simply abandoned, text-based opportunities for talk are not seized.

Pat's metaphor—going "far afield" and then "pulling back in"—suggests her way of dealing with this potential problem. The talk moves away from the book *and then moves back to it;* it ebbs and flows. Pat is often (but by no means always) the one who brings the discussion back to the text, but she is careful not to interrupt the movement away; rather, she waits for the outward surge to end and then asks a more text-related question that brings things inward. She waits for a juncture in the conversation when she can initiate a shift without shutting off talk on a topic that is still warm.

In a discussion of *Arthur's April Fool* (Brown, 1985), Tommy told two stories about tricking his parents on April Fools' Day. The second went like this:

Tommy: I told my mom, "Can I tell you what toy I want to get?" and she said, "OK." So me and her went to Toys "Я" Us and there were these little toys that my mommy picked and I said, "I want a plastic spider." And she looked all over the store and she couldn't find it and I said, "April Fool."

Martin: Oh, no. You did that trick all the way to Toys "Я" Us?

Tommy: Yeah. [*Pat laughs.*] And I looked at the other toys for a long time. But there was one little plastic spider that she was about to get but somebody took it.

By this point, Tommy's turn had been devoted almost entirely to these trickster stories. Pat noted in the margin of the transcript, "I decided to move the discussion back to the book for a few minutes before we went on to the next person." So, keeping to Tommy's topic of tricks, she asked:

Pat: Do you think this was a good joke that Arthur played on Binky Barnes?

Tommy [*indicating yes*]: And I know how Arthur did it.

Then, as Tommy tried to tell about Arthur's tricks, Pat used supporting language to help him along.

Tommy: He wanted to be strong like this. He went through all these things.

Pat: All these magazines.

Tommy: And he wanted to be this guy.

Pat: Mr. America.

Tommy: He acted like he was really tough. But he wasn't.

Pat: He can't really make himself bigger than Binky Barnes.

We can see this same pattern of movement back toward the text in this excerpt from a discussion of *Arthur's Nose* (Brown, 1976).

Arthur has visited the rhinologist and can choose from an array of noses. Jake had asked, "Of these pictures, what nose would you pick?"

Jed: I would say—

Jake: I would say the mouse.

Jed: I got three. I like the hippopotamus, the alligator, and the rhinoceros.

Jake: I would take the alligator, the mouse, and the rabbit.

Jed: I like the rhinoceros. It's so big. Adam.

Adam: I'd pick the alligator.

Jake: I would, too.

Jed: Mrs. McLure.

Sensing that the deciding had come to an end, Pat shifted back to Arthur's decision not to pick any of the noses.

Pat: Why does Arthur decide to keep his own nose?

Jed: Well, let's see [*looks at pages*]. Well, he just thought he wasn't him without his nose. Well, I'm not me without my nose. I wouldn't want to come into class with an alligator nose or a rhinoceros nose.

In this and many other discussions, the outward movement assisted the inward movement. Jed could imagine Arthur's situation because he and the other members spent so much time mentally trying on noses.

Paradoxically, when the members of the groups were unable to move outward from the text, they had difficulty moving back into it. The story never became contextualized, never linked to their lives in any significant way. This was the case in a sharing session on yet another *Arthur* book, *Arthur's Valentine* (Brown, 1985), which Sandy shared. Adam responded by asking Sandy to relate the story to her experience.

Adam: What did you get for Valentine's last year?

Sandy: Some candy and a lot of valentines [*pauses for ten seconds*]. I can't remember that much.

Normally, this question would lead to Valentine's Day stories, but here—nothing. A few exchanges later, Pat tried to shift to the children's experiences drawing things in the snow.

Pat: have you ever drawn things in the snow?
Sandy: Yeah, like numbers and letters.
Pat: Mm-hm.

Here she offered a cue to Sandy to go on, but Sandy didn't expand. Pat turned to Melanie.

Pat: Do you do that?
Melanie: No.
Pat: No?

Again, a verbal cue to continue, which Melanie did not pick up on. Pat shifted the topic back to Valentine's Day.

Pat: Do you know when Valentine's Day is?
Sandy: Uh-uh.
Cindy: The fourteenth.
Pat: When is that?

Things were not going well—and they got no better. In the transcript, I wrote, "Pat, you seem to be doing more question asking than usual, right? Was it because other kids had trouble getting into Sandy's story?"

Pat answered, "Yes. It's surprising that they didn't start talking about snowball fights, playing in the snow, Valentine's Day—there were plenty of topics to take off with." This lack of connection seemed to foreclose all talk on the book. And because there was no chain of associations, where children talked to children, Pat was thrown back on a role she usually managed to avoid, that of the primary questioner who takes every other turn.

Relating Texts

Just as students can move outward from a text in order to tell personal stories, they can move outward from it to talk about similar published books. To go back to the campfire metaphor, those sitting around the fire include not only the author of the book shared and the students; the group includes other published authors as well, more and more as the year progresses.

Pat never modeled the "that reminds me" move toward a related personal story—she didn't have to—and she very rarely told personal stories in the groups. But she did use the "that reminds me" link to talk about published books, sometimes giving a discussion a second life in this way. In a share session on *Amelia Bedelia and the Baby* (Parish, 1982), Pat asked if any of the members had read books where words have different meanings.

Abby: Yeah.

Pat: Have you ever seen that book called *The King Who Rained* [Gwynne, 1988]?

Abby: Oooh. Yeah.

Pat: Where words have two different meanings.

Abby: Yeah, yeah. "Have you ever seen such a bunch of fairy tails?"

Scott: "Did you ever see such a bunch of fairy tails?"

Pat: Tails instead of stories. Yeah. And the one about forks in the road. Instead of eating forks.

Abby: Oooh. Like the king rained. Or the "coat of arms."

Pat: Yeah, "the coat of arms."

And so on for a couple more minutes. On this and many other occasions, Pat functioned as a resource, someone who knows the books in the class and knows what students are reading. Students are constantly being reminded of the range of possibilities for choosing.

Sometimes in the whole group sessions, Pat shared different versions of the same folktale, which students then contrasted. There is a close parallel here between the folk culture of the class and the folktales they hear. When they tell associated stories, they seem to tell versions of the tooth-fairy story, the finding-the-Easter-egg story, the skunk story, the photocopying story, with each turn adding a new twist. It is a small step to discussions such as the following, in which the class talked about different versions of *The Three Little Pigs.*

Rob: Well, I have another version and the first pig builds his house out of grass. And the second builds his out of cardboard and the third built his house out of stones.

Melanie: Stones, stones, stones are the best.

Rob: But he doesn't have a chimney so he makes like a group of stones and he puts a little fire in front of the doorway, and when the Big Bad Wolf opens the door he gets burned in the fire.

Martin: One time I watched Bugs Bunny and they had a version like when the wolf couldn't blow down the brick house, Bugs Bunny helped because the wolf couldn't blow down the house. When the wolf blew you saw a big cloud of smoke so Bugs Bunny took some dynamite and he blew the house up. And the wolf thought he did it.

Melanie mentioned the version where the wolf tries to trick the pigs into going apple picking. And, finally, Cindy told about a version— the sixth, counting the book being shared—in which the second little pig has a girlfriend.

The word *version* became part of the students' critical vocabulary, and well it should have. For they were constantly telling versions, writing versions, and reading versions. No text in this class existed singly. They were all turns in a yearlong conversation.

Being "Teacher"

In *Living Between the Lines* (1991), Lucy Calkins tells a story of a school in which a number of boys were writing about farts. The teachers, true to writing-process orthodoxy, gave students a free rein in topic choice. When Mary Ellen Giacobbe was called in as a consultant, teachers asked her what to do when the boys wrote about farts. "Tell them to stop," she said. Of course. But the emphasis on allowing students to direct their own learning (sometimes stated as a directive—let students choose their own topics) can easily be read as a prohibition on any teacher direction that might deny a child's "ownership" of the process.

Similarly, in Pat's class, students have considerable freedom to initiate and shift topics of conversation (though not to farts). But, at times, Pat can become "the teacher." She does not take this more directive role often, but it is a part of her repertoire that she uses when students are missing key information or when she feels more active questioning is needed to draw a student out. A small example is the following exchange near the end of a discussion of *Spectacles* by Ellen Raskin (1968).

Pat: The title of this one. That word you had trouble with. Do you know what that means?

Jake: No.

Pat: Does anybody?

Joyce: Glasses.

Pat: Yes, glasses. Spectacles is another word for glasses.

Here the discussion shifted to the initiate-respond-evaluate pattern that Mehan (1979) describes as characteristic of much classroom talk. Pat's decision to shift into this didactic mode was based on the difficulty that Jake had with the word. It was not a decision made in advance of the reading, as it would be in a traditional reading lesson.

In some cases, she takes on the teacherly role when she sees that students lack the background they need to understand a text fully. In September, Cindy shared *Stop* by Joy Cowley (1981), a beginning reading book in which a milkman delivering milk apparently forgets to put his emergency brake on and his truck goes backward. The text on almost every page takes the form: " 'Stop,' said the ———. But the truck wouldn't stop." Sandy asked why the truck wouldn't stop.

Cindy: I don't know. I guess there's no driver.

Jake: He didn't put his brakes on.

Cindy: I don't know if there is any driver. See [*pointing to the book*], there's no driver.

Jake: Ah, I guess he didn't put on his brakes or his brakes didn't work.

Cindy: See, that is the milkman and I guess he was thrown out or something. I don't know.

At this point, it occurred to Pat that Cindy and perhaps other members of the group did not know what a milkman does. Her clue was that Cindy had figured out that the milkman being out of the truck was part of the problem but she wasn't sure why he was out.

Pat: Do you know what a milkman does?
Cindy: Well, I guess he drives around and delivers milk to people.
Pat: Do you have a milkman?
Cindy: No.

But Abby did have a milkman, and she told what she knew, and Sandy, who had seen a milk truck come to her cousin's house, told her story, too. Pat then continued.

Pat: When the milkman brings the new milk to the house, in this picture he's picking up the empty bottles. Why do you suppose he is doing that?
Cindy: I don't know.
Pat: That's what people used to do when they had a milkman. They put out the empty bottles, and then they take them back and wash them out and fill them up with new milk.
Jake: Is it like a glass bottle or a plastic bottle?
Pat: It was a glass bottle.

At this point, Cindy *seemed* to have dropped out of the conversation. But this talk of what happens on a milk delivery finally clarified for her what is happening in the picture. Now, four minutes after Sandy asked why the truck didn't stop, Cindy had an answer.

Cindy [*excited*]: See I just noticed. These are new milks. These are new milks. These are new milks, and he's delivering those but he forgot to stop the truck so it's going on the road.
Pat: That's right, it took off without the driver.
Cindy: Yeah.

Again, in a traditional reading lesson, this background information on milk delivery typically would be presented before the story. Pat, however, took the cue from Cindy's answer that home milk delivery was unfamiliar to some students.

Listening In

A third way in which Pat takes a teacherly role is to become the active questioner when the student presenting a book does not seem to respond to the questions from group members. Allan, a quiet, slow-spoken second grader, often needed to be pushed a bit to show what he understood about a book. One day, he shared *Ramona and Her Mother* (Cleary, 1990), summarizing the chapter where Ramona wears her red pajamas to school, but, when he read aloud, he didn't get to the pajama part. Pat, uncharacteristically, was the first to pose a question.

Pat: Um, in the part you read to us you didn't get to the part about her wearing the pajamas to school.
Allan: No.
Pat: That part comes later in the chapter?
Allan: Yeah.
Pat: Why did she take her pajamas to school?
Allan: I don't know.

By this point, Pat had received three nonresponses to her questions. But, convinced that Allan *did* know the answer, she asked again.

Pat: Did she take them or did she just wear them?
Allan: She weared them because she felt so snug and she didn't want to change them.
Pat: Ohhh. How did she get home without them?
Allan: She brought some clothes to school, and she changes in the girl's bathroom.

Pat pressed Allan in a similar way in the discussion on *The Teacher from the Black Lagoon* (Thaler, 1989) quoted in chapter 5. As you recall, the talk centered on the plausibility of the monster scenes in the book. Scott thought that the whole thing was a dream. Allan, however, disagreed.

Allan: I don't think so. Because it's his first day at school and I don't think he would be dreaming in school, on the first day of school.

132

Scott: Well, maybe that is his dream from his nap.

At this point, there was a five-second pause; Allan did not come up with an alternate explanation for the bizarre events in the story. Scott changed the subject.

Scott [*pointing to a picture*]: What's this?
Allan: It's "Mrs. Jones has a wig and a whip." Any more comments or
    questions.

Here, seeing that Scott's observation was in danger of being abandoned, Pat stepped in.

Pat: Well, how do you think the story goes then? You don't think he
    was dreaming?
Allan: No.
Pat: How do you think all those ideas came to him about those
    teachers?
Allan: I don't know.
Pat: Who was telling him about those teachers? How did he find out?
Allan: I don't know. Well, at the picture I was drawing he's looking at
    a paper that tells all the teachers and what they have.
Pat: So he's the first one in the classroom.
Allan: Yeah.
Pat: All by himself.
Allan: Now I think he's dreaming.
Pat: What makes you think so?
Allan: Because he's closing his eyes.

Pat was not grilling Allan, despite the impression this bare transcript gives. Her voice was gentle, curious, but insistent.

    The teacherly interventions that I've noted in this section all entail risks. Students may talk less. They may try to please authority. In situations like the one above, some students might feel singled out and exposed. And, as we all know, when we see ourselves as the primary questioner, we may become more intent on what we say, on our next questions, than on what students say. Yet there are risks in nonintervention, too. Jake might never have understood the title of the book he shared. Cindy might never have understood the way milkmen exchange old bottles for "new milks." Allan might have appeared a far less competent reader and thinker.

In the Oliver North hearing before the Congressional investigatory committee, North's lawyer, Brendan Sullivan, was reprimanded for being too aggressive. Sullivan shot back, "I'm not a potted plant." Neither are teachers—though some descriptions of process class-rooms suggest as much. Too often, the idea of authority or control is treated as a fixed-sum game; that is, as though there is a fixed quantity of something called authority, let's say 100 points of it. If the student is to have more authority (say 50 points), the teacher has to reduce his or her authority by the same amount. Whatever happens, the sum must total 100. It is as if the nature of authority does not change in a process classroom, only the proportions of it assigned to teacher and students. Whatever the case, the teacher may need to retain some points—just in case students write about farts.

I don't believe authority works like this. Pat is a major influence in the sharing group, as I've tried to show in this chapter. She is not just a peer, and she's definitely not a potted plant. She is attuned to critical junctures in the talk where she sees a need to enter in. And at times she will become dominant, didactic. But her involvement does not preclude opportunities for students to influence the group—indeed, I believe it actually enhances them. Her effectiveness is due to her ability to read a conversation, to read a situation, and to use her authority with a light touch.

9

"I Don't Always Tell Them What They Want to Hear"

FOR A WORKSHOP, Pat asked her students to draw the activity centers in the room. The child who chose to draw the center table, where the share groups take place, drew four children, their books in front of them, paper and a cup of pencils in the center of the table. It is an exact picture with one significant exception—Pat isn't in it.

The children see Pat more as a recorder than as a participant in the discussion (though, as I showed in the last chapter, her participation is significant). In her loose-leaf binder, she keeps an approximate stenographic record of each share session. By the end of the year, her accumulated transcripts of these sessions amount to over fifty thousand words, a record longer than this book. She keeps similar records of the whole-class share sessions, and these fill another binder. By the end of the year, for each child, she has approximately 60 narrative records of sharing sessions. If a child has been with her for two years, she has made 120 accounts (about twelve thousand words, the equivalent of forty-eight typed pages).

Her records of the sharing sessions are unanalyzed accounts of what is said (the analysis comes later, when she writes up her individual reports). Each one includes the title and author of the book, the child's summary of the book, and the questions and answers in the share group. In addition, she may also note observations about the fluency or expressiveness of the reading, the miscues or substitutions in the reading, who in the group offers help with difficult words, and actions that accompany reading (e.g., sound effects).

These abbreviated records give a clear picture of the talk that occurs. Here, for example, is her record of a session at which Allan shared the ever-popular *Arthur's Halloween* (Brown, 1982).

> It's about an anteater and he has to go trick or treating with his baby sister—and they take the graveyard route home and Arthur makes a joke—Allan shows us silhouette picture in the graveyard and tells us each character's name—Reads—Have you read lots of other Arthur books—Yes—starts to tell us then checks list of titles in back of book—I remember last Halloween the HH [Haunted House] that was in the gym and I think Tommy's uncle was there and I felt the eyeballs, brains, and hearts just like in here. Abby—we are trying to grow a giant pumpkin and my grandpa gives it a can of beer every day

Joyce—fav. Arthur—*Arthur's Nose*—because Arthur tries out the rhino nose and it's too big—Joyce—Last year we carved out a pumpkin like a penguin—Halloween stories.

In the record of a share group on Arthur Yorinks's *Company's Coming* (1988), a session I transcribed, Pat captured the enjoyment that Jake and the group felt as they rekindled the funny parts of the book. In it, aliens come to give a blender as a housewarming present and are met by massed weaponry.

This book is about two people and there is one in the yard and another in the house and one day a flying saucer comes by and lands in the yard and their names are Moe and Shirley. Then the space creatures walk out. Jake imitates space creatures—Jed—I thought it was funny when they were so scared and they were giving them a blender—Reads the part he thinks is really neat—corrects himself when he misses a period—Vicky—That was funny—"Do you have a bathroom." Jed—what was that big thing—It looked like a jet—It's either a bomb or a missile— Me—So they never have anything to worry about—No, not really—Sandy fav. jet—look at illus—I think I like all of them but I do like one helicopter—Adam—Would you like to be one of those aliens—I wouldn't if I was visiting Earth with all those machine guns—

If the oral reading is relatively fluent, Pat may make no comment about decoding or oral expression. But when children experience difficulty, she notes this in her transcripts.

She is a capable reader—yet it's hard to know what she uses— she asks for help with "wicker" but reads "containing." Pronounces "liked" as two-syllable word—like-ed, jump-ed, laugh-ed, ask-ed. Leans to Corrine for help—lay, waiting, shirt, heard, door.

These notations are not as specific as the running record that would be kept by teachers in the Reading Recovery program; she does not note, for example, all repetitions, self-corrections, and rereadings unless they significantly affect the reading. Pat also notes when the oral reading is especially good.

Great reading—he has practiced.

Good reading with expression.

In addition to providing a splendid record of the talk in the groups, the very act of making these notations focuses Pat on what the children say. This stenographic task also limits her own talking in the groups because of the difficulty in talking and taking notes at the same time.

It's late April, and the chicks project is coming to a close. Pat is sick of them. She shows me a newly hatched chick that has been separated from the hen and other baby chicks and put in an emptied aquarium. "He must have been pecked by accident and once the other chicks saw blood they went after him. The kids were really upset. So we had to put him in the aquarium, and he wasn't happy there by himself, so we put a mirror in. Now he thinks he sees another chick so he's a little more content."

Pat is beginning to write the reports she will present to the parents of these students, and she has agreed to walk me through the one on Cindy. I sit with her at the round central table with her notebooks of transcriptions before her. "I read all of the times she's shared, what she's shared, how she's responded. I go to the files and look at the last report I wrote. I want to notice anything different in terms of reading choices, anything particular to the child. Cindy's read three or four alphabet books, a couple by Jerry Pelotta, and she just did a bird alphabet book. And she's often the first reader of new books in the classroom."

Pat's comments remind me that she has described the transcripts as the raw material for the "reading history" that she is trying to piece out for each child. I ask her to define what she means by "reading history."

"It's more than one thing. In some respects, it's the style of going about reading. Someone like Scott would chew into something that was too difficult. Part of his history is the way he has always gone about challenging himself, diving into things that were really hard,

139

floundering through it, but figuring a lot about reading along the way. Others will choose some things that they can be fairly independent with and move through reading that way.

"And the other part of the history is what they've read. All that background of what kinds of things they've been exposed to. They build up a history of all their past readings. I also think it's important for them to talk about these histories. The more they think about things they've read before, it helps them find other things they might like to read. Or it helps them recommend books to other people. That just shuffles all around the room. Everybody gets touched by different books that way."

One of Cindy's favorite author illustrators is Barbara Cooney. In the past summer, she and Abby met Barbara Cooney at a reading in Durham. Pat reads from a conversation between Cindy and Abby.

Abby: Remember when we saw Barbara Cooney last year? There was this long, long line of teachers and they just let us go up to the front.

Cindy: I know. My secret to getting through was just being a cute little kid.

"Another thing I'm looking for is organization, how they plan out their reading. Cindy plans it out. I noticed a couple of examples: when she shared valentine poems by Jack Prelutsky she said, 'It had a lot of funny Valentine's Day poems, some short, some long. I'll read two.' And when she read *Animalia* by Graeme Base [1987], she said, 'It has really neat things because you have to find things that start with the letter. And you have to find Graeme Base on every page, and I'll show you Graeme Base.'

"Sometimes she had a hard time summarizing. A book like *Island Boy* [Cooney, 1988] or *Princess Furball* [Huck, 1989] is hard to summarize. But in terms of the report, I won't write about her having difficulty—it's a hard task. And by what she is telling us she shows she is understanding.

"I'll probably say something about her oral reading being expressive. With her, reading is really clicking into place. She has experience with books. She knows how language sounds. She uses dialogue in her writing and knows how to use punctuation to guide her oral reading." Cindy showed this familiarity with book language in her story *The Boring Adventure,* in which she and Abby were main characters. An excerpt:

> They were in Sweden skiing down mountains. "Boring," said Cindy.
> And then they were back in the Colleseum. "Boring," said Cindy.
> Then they took this plane to Alaska and they got chased by a walrus. "Boring," said Cindy.

As the class picked up on the structure of the book, they chimed in on each repetition of "boring."

Before Pat began her reports, she surveyed students to see what they saw themselves as experts in. Cindy claimed she was good at "writing funny stories." Then Pat asked each student in the class to say what every other member of the class was an expert in. The most common answer for Cindy was that she was good at soccer, particularly at being goalie. She was the only girl from the class who played with the boys. They also mentioned her sewing (she learned cross-stitch and showed some classmates how to do it during free-choice time). And Abby said that Cindy was good at "being a friend."

Every child is an expert. I thought of the reassurance that this assumption provides to parents in this district. I thought of how each parent, myself included, craves that mark of exceptionality. Pat and I sometimes joke about sporadic efforts to set up a Gifted and Talented Program in the district. "How could they keep anyone out? How would you like the job of explaining to parents that their kid didn't make it?"

I ask Pat how she sees her role as writer of these annual reports. "I try to include enough about the child so I could block out the name and I would know who it was—by learning style, choices, what they see or what I see as their expertise. I just want the report to be specific. It should point out the real strengths, and the transcripts help me make it personal to that child." Here is the language arts section of her report on Cindy.

> Cindy's choices for reading and writing reflect her variety of interests. She says her favorites are alphabet books and fairy tales. During the year, she has read several alphabet books

including *Animalia* by Graeme Base, *Zoophabets* by Robert Tallon, and a couple by Jerry Pallota. She seemed particularly pleased with the new one by Anita Lobel that she received for her birthday.

Princess Furball by Charlotte Huck is one of the fairy tales that Cindy read this year. She brought the book to a small group for discussion, and she also shared it with the whole class. When she introduced the book in the small group, she began with a brief summary of the characters and plot before choosing a part of the book to read aloud. She tells us, "I am going to read until they find her." I have noticed that Cindy often plans ahead for her sharing times. She understands that time is a factor so she thinks about which parts of the story she would most like to read aloud.

Because most of our discussion and Cindy's reading had focused on the beginning of the story, I asked her how the story ended. She related it to another fairy tale when she answered, "Well, it sort of ends like Cinderella. She's working for the cook in the royal kitchen and she asks if she can go to the ball. . . . She dances with the prince . . . and they live happily ever after."

Cindy's reading and writing and her interest in art are coming together in her recent project about Van Gogh. Following a trip to the Museum of Fine Arts, she started reading a book about Vincent Van Gogh, and then she started to write her own book about the artist. She has experimented with some materials to try to reproduce some of his paintings and she shared her work with the class. She plans to publish her book before the end of the year.

Pat's report is interesting in both what it does and what it does not say. Her comments focus on bedrock principles in her teaching—the importance of planning, of choosing books, of being able effectively to "say a few words about the book," of being able to summarize texts, of relating art, reading, and writing. But there are silences, too. I ask Pat about them.

"There's a kind of statement that I think you would not make. 'It was a real pleasure to have your son in class' or 'It was a joy to have your son in class.' "

"Sometimes I do on the very last one I'm writing for someone, like for some of the second graders."

"But why not in the earlier ones?"

"I don't know that it's saying that much about the child's work in the room or progress in the room. What does it matter whether I enjoyed working with them? That's my job. That's what I'm here to do. And it probably comes through in the way I talk about the child."

"Another comment that I expect you would never write is something like—'your child is an exceptional reader.'"

"Right. I wouldn't write something like that. I might use 'very capable' but that's the farthest I'll go."

"Why?"

"Well, I see it as a form of grading, like embedding the grade in the report. I know some parents want that. They'll come into conference and say, 'I know you don't give grades but if you did what grade would my child get?' So I hem and haw and sidestep and try to explain that each individual has a set of strengths that I try to describe. Or they come with the report I've written and then set it aside, look at me, and say, "Now how's she really doing?"

Pat paused. "I don't always tell them what they want to hear."

What do they (we) want to hear? I think about that question as I look across the Mast Way playing fields to the bleachers where, in the early evening, parents watch with special intensity as their children play T-ball. They want to hear that their children have a special relationship with their teacher. They want to hear that their child is excelling. But isn't one person's excellence another's relative failure? Isn't competition implicit in these parents' concept of excellence? Hasn't it been central to their own achievements? To be excellent is to be superior to others. Can you have winners without losers?

Pat's refusal even to use a term like "exceptional" is a quiet act of defiance. The silences in her report testify to her rejection of norming students, of separating winners and losers. She is even silent about her relationship with the students. Like the child who drew the activity center, Pat does not put herself in the picture.

10

Who Will Live
in This House?

A FEW YEARS ago, my family moved into a new house. We had been living in what real estate agents call a starter home. It was usually a mess—cobwebs, windows that went years without cleaning, the floor littered with a week's worth of the *Boston Globe*. We respected the force of gravity; if something fell on the floor, we left it there. Sometime in April each year, we'd say, "Now this year we're going to do a spring cleaning." But we never did.

Then we began looking at newer houses. They were spotless. The sun streamed in through clean windows. There were no magic marker scrawls on the walls. The floors were carpeted, sometimes so thick our feet sank in. A pewter chandelier hung above the dining room table. In this house, I thought, we'd be a different family. I imagined us all sitting down to a calm and stately dinner, maybe with Vivaldi playing in the background. I imagined us in the living room in the early evening, the kids stretched out on the plush carpet reading Caldecott and Newbery Medal books. I imagined us transformed.

There was only one problem. It was still the Newkirks that would be living in this house. The same Newkirks that hated to pick up (let alone clean). We would be the ones living in that house.

We bought a house and pretty soon our new, more elegant house came to resemble the old one. Cobwebs formed. My son still insisted on keeping his school clothes on the living room floor. Still no spring cleaning. There was no transformation.

As teachers, many of us now have an opportunity to enter a new house. We can live in the house of whole language. We can get rid of rows of seats. We can designate an Author's Chair. We can fill the house with children's literature. We can bring in writing and reading folders to be filled with drafts and reading journals.

But who will live in this house? We will. And if we bring along our traditional habits of overtalking and underlistening, this new house may, after a while, end up looking like the ones we left.

Transformation, if it is to happen, can only come through self-study. And paradoxically, talk, because it is such a regular and "natural" activity, eludes examination. Nothing is so intimate, literally so close to us, as our voice—yet we are surprised to hear it on tape (am I that nasal?) or to read transcripts (did I talk that much?). Trying to hear our own talk is like a game I used to play with my kids. They would climb onto my back, and I would "try to find them." I would say, "I know you're here. I know you're close." I would turn and, of course, could never find them because they were always behind me.

I hope that this extended study of talk in one classroom will aid self-study. Pat's discussion groups are not presented as models for all teachers; they reflect her goals and draw from her personality. They carry her signature. But I hope that, by attending to this classroom, by listening attentively, we can help make talk in our classrooms more audible. By attending to Pat's decisions, we can reflect upon our own; by listening to her silences, we can become aware of our own. Whether this attention moves us to become more like her is irrelevant.

In many ways, I am the primary beneficiary of this study. In the hours of recording, the days of transcribing, I came to understand a way of being with students that was radically different from my own. In the rest of this chapter, I want to reflect on how this difference has caused me to rethink my own approaches to teaching.

We can begin with the relationship of teacher talk to ego. I don't mean ego in a negative sense; rather, I'm talking about our common need to maintain a sense of our own competence and the way we all act, consciously or unconsciously, to meet that need. One way we do this is by talking. We can feel competent if we are interesting, motivating, funny. I come out of a class wondering "How did I do?" which really means "How well did I talk?" Underlying this concern is the model of the charismatic teacher that we (or at least I) still cling to. The charismatic teacher inspires through self-presentation, and that means through talk (Robin Williams in *The Dead Poet's Society,* for example). My guess is that many of us who have tried to empower students still retain, at some level, a desire to be that charismatic leader.

Pat's approach is resolutely anticharismatic. She rarely places herself in the foreground, rarely tells her own stories during share time, and, when she does speak, she tends not to initiate but to react. She is clearly more a listener than a speaker. Listening to her for a year made me aware of how the charismatic model can get in the way. Sometimes, particularly when I speak too long and too emphatically, my talk works against student participation. The charismatic model pushes me to try to be impressive when more tentative comments might make for more sustained discussion. The charismatic model pushes me to make minispeeches that can bring a string of talk to an end. More subtly, the charismatic model directs my attention to myself, my performance, and away from what students are doing and saying.

In the end, Pat's silences define her teaching style. Time after time, as the talk moved unpredictably from topic to topic, leaving the book far behind, I tried to second-guess when she would come in. I would pick the spot where *I* would move the talk back to the book, when I would redirect it with a question. But she would let it go on. I once asked her how she could be so patient, and she looked at me quizzically and said, "I don't think of it as patient. I'm interested in what they say." Of course. She couldn't be gritting her teeth, trying to hold back. She wouldn't have any teeth left.

The waiting, the nonintervention, didn't always pay off. One reader of this manuscript claimed that there were "teachable moments" that she missed. I'm sure he is right. But as an observer, I became acutely aware of what a quick trigger finger I have had during class discussions. Too often when talk seemed to move off topic, I would begin to shift in my seat and at the first opportunity try to yank it back, just as I do when my dog stops on the better-kept Durham lawns. I now see how the digressions in Pat's class, and in my own, can help to contextualize issues or readings; they can be a journey outward, into the lives of students, that can allow a journey further inward, back to the topic or text. Rather than stopping these digressions, I now realize I need to push them, to encourage students to construct that network of stories.

Though I still call these journeys outward "digressions," it is important to remember that, for Pat, they are not digressions. It took me months to realize that. And in order to understand her attitude, I had to understand her concept of community. I assumed I understood the central place of community or collaboration in reading/writing-process classrooms. I understood that the whole-language movement was a challenge to the concept of solitary learning where the only relationship students had was competitive. I understood all that.

But I still tended to view collaboration as a means to an end, believing that students needed the help of others only so that they could reach their potential as learners. To borrow from Vygotsky

149

(1978), what they can do in cooperation today, they will be able to do individually in the future. Writers and readers need feedback if they are to improve their work, and the community provides this structured support. I knew all that.

But, for Pat, collaboration is not simply a means to an end. It is an end in itself. At times, it even seemed that literacy was a means of engendering collaboration, rather than the reverse. For example, when Phillip read one of his space stories in class, I would instinctively focus on qualities of the story and ways it could be made better. Pat, while not neglecting these literary issues, would see the story as an indication of how the boy network in her class was working. Who was Phillip involving in his story? Which of the boys (or girls) seemed responsive to his story? How did his story build on the storytelling of others in the class? It was as if she saw the story as the scene where relationships were worked out.

Pat's sense of community resembles that of teachers in the laboratory school established by John Dewey in the 1890s. In an address to parents, Dewey described the communal spirit of the school.

> As regards the spirit of the school, the chief object is to secure a free and informal community life in which each child will feel that he has a share and his own work to do. This is made the chief motive toward what is ordinarily termed order and discipline. (Quoted in Mayhew and Edwards, [1936] 1966, 32)

The growth of the school, according to Dewey, depended on what he called "coeducation," which involved breaking down divisions between those who taught and those who learned.

> There is one kind of coeducation to which no one makes objections—one which is absolutely indispensable if the future of this school is to be as significant as its own past exacts of it. This is coeducation of teachers, students, and parents by one another. (15)

This spirit of coeducation animated the reading share groups and every other learning center of the classroom. For Dewey (and for Pat), the capacity to contribute to a community was not a set of social skills to be checked on the backside of a report card. Sense of community was central to his (and her) vision of democracy and to the school's role in instilling democratic values.

Pat's focus on communal relationships is quietly subversive. On her narrative reports, she refused to provide those normative statements of achievement (e.g., "your child is an exceptional reader") that parents crave. I also came to see that some of the most valued moments in her classroom were not those of individual achievement. They were moments of cooperative excellence: when Joyce gently showed Melanie the routines for sharing in the small group; when Cindy showed the class how to cross-stitch; when a group of boys negotiated who would be on which space ship and how they would escape.

The more I thought about the value system that informed Pat's view of her students, the more radical, even heretical, it appeared to me. It is heretical because it goes against one central belief that, curiously, unites skills-based and whole-language instruction in reading and writing: that literacy development should be the focus of elementary school instruction (by contrast, Dewey's laboratory school gave little attention to reading). The proverbial visitor from another planet would surely conclude that this country thinks literacy learning is difficult. Why else would we spend billions of dollars on literacy education and support a massive corps of reading specialists, remedial teachers, and an immense textbook and professional publication industry? Social development would be viewed by this visitor either as unimportant or as a natural endowment, easily acquired outside the school.

By contrast, Japanese parents think that reading is easily taught at home but that children need to go to school to develop a capacity to work in groups.

> Although reading can be readily taught at home most Japanese parents today feel that character can be properly developed only at school. To grow up exclusively in the bosom of a nuclear family is to risk not becoming truly Japanese, to risk being too self-centered and too dyadic rather than group oriented in one's interpersonal relations. Japanese parents sent their children to preschool not just for child care and not just so the children can learn to modify their behavior to conform to

151

demands of society but, more profoundly, to facilitate the development of a group-oriented, outward-facing sense of self. (Tobin, Wu, and Davidson, 1989, 58)

I believe that, for Pat, the development of this "group-oriented, outward-facing sense of self" is central to her goals, and she is alert to indications of communal excellence. It took me a long time to see that.

If I learned one central lesson in writing this book, it was the importance of keeping track of talk. One day in late June, after school had let out for the summer, I stopped by Pat's room to pick up the last transcript. She was on an errand in the office, so I sat in the still classroom for a few minutes waiting for her . In the unnatural quiet, it struck me that had we not recorded those conversations in notes and transcripts, all of it would have been lost. For what had we studied? Vibrations in the air, nothing more. I wondered what happened to those vibrations—are there still traces, infinitesimal quivers, out there somewhere?

If there are, they are irretrievable. The talk, virtually all of it, is gone, and for a few minutes I felt the poignancy of this loss. The life of this class was the talk—Billy's craziness, Abby's cat stories, Michelle's brother stories, talk of mousetraps and Mexican jumping beans and Tic-Tacs. I began to think that the reason we don't study talk is that it reminds us of our own mortality, our inability to hold on to the moments of our lives. No wonder we prefer the stability of print with its illusion of permanence.

But we had caught a sliver of it, however stripped of sound and gesture, and from that sliver we formed this book. It is offered not as a model to be followed but as an invitation to listen in, to record, preserve, and reflect on these wondrous vibrations of air.

References

AHLBERG, ALLAN. *Funnybones.* 1981. New York: Greenwillow.

ALLARD, HARRY, AND JAMES MARSHALL. 1977. *The Stupids Step Out.* Boston: Houghton Mifflin.

———. 1981. *The Stupids Die.* Boston: Houghton Mifflin.

APPLEBEE, ARTHUR. 1978. *The Child's Concept of Story: Ages Two to Seventeen.* Chicago: University of Chicago Press.

AVERILL, ESTHER. 1960. *The Fire Cat.* New York: Harper.

BARRETT, JUDI. 1978. *Cloudy with a Chance of Meatballs.* New York: Atheneum.

BARTHOLOMAE, DAVID. 1986. "Wanderings: Misreadings, Miswritings, Misunderstandings." In *Only Connect: Uniting Reading and Writing,* ed. Thomas Newkirk. Portsmouth, N.H.: Heinemann/Boynton Cook.

BASE, GRAEME. 1987. *Animalia.* New York: Harry Abrams.

BERNSTEIN, BASIL. 1966. "A Critique of the Concept of 'Compensatory Education.'" In *Education for Democracy,* ed. Rubinstein and Stoneman. Harmondsworth, England: Penguin.

BLACKBURN, ELLEN. 1984. "Common Ground: Developing Relationships Between Reading and Writing." *Language Arts* 61:367–75.

BRIDWELL, NORMAN. 1984. *Clifford's ABC's.* New York: Scholastic.

———. 1984. *Clifford's Christmas.* New York: Scholastic.

———. 1984. *Clifford's Family.* New York: Scholastic.

———. 1984. *Clifford's Kitten.* New York: Scholastic.

———. 1984. *Clifford's Riddles.* New York: Scholastic.

———. 1984. *Clifford's Sticker Book.* New York: Scholastic.

BROOKE, ROBERT. 1987. "Underlife and Writing Instruction." *College Composition and Communication* 38:141–53.

BROWN, MARC. 1985. *Arthur's April Fool.* Boston: Houghton Mifflin.

———. 1985. *Arthur's Tooth.* Boston: Houghton Mifflin.

———. 1985. *Arthur's Valentine.* Boston: Houghton Mifflin.

———. 1982. *Arthur's Halloween.* Boston: Houghton Mifflin.

———. 1976. *Arthur's Nose.* Boston: Houghton Mifflin.

BRUNER, JEROME. 1985. *Child's Talk: Learning to Use Language.* New York: Norton.

CALHOUN, MARY. 1988. *Cross-Country Cat.* New York: Morrow.

———. 1981. *Hot Air Henry.* New York: Morrow.

CALKINS, LUCY MCCORMICK. 1991. *Living Between the Lines.* Portsmouth, N.H.: Heinemann.

CARLE, ERIC. 1990. *Pancakes, Pancakes.* Saxonville, N.Y.: Picture Book Studios.

———. 1989. *A Very Busy Spider.* New York: Putnam.

———. 1981. *A Very Hungry Caterpillar.* New York: Putnam.

CARTER, MICHAEL. 1990. "The Idea of Expertise: An Exploration of Cognitive and Social Dimensions of Writing." *College Composition and Communication* 41:265–86.

CAZDEN, COURTNEY. 1988. *Classroom Discourse: The Language of Teaching and Learning.* Portsmouth, N.H.: Heinemann.

CLEARY, BEVERLY. 1990. *Ramona and Her Mother.* New York: Avon.

———. 1985. *Ramona Forever.* New York: Dell.

———. 1981. *Runaway Ralph.* New York: Dell.

———. 1980. *The Mouse and the Motorcycle.* New York: Dell.

COLE, JOANNA. 1986. *The Magic School Bus at the Waterworks.* New York: Scholastic.

COOK, BERNADINE. 1956. *The Little Fish That Got Away.* New York: W.R. Scott.

References

COONEY, BARBARA. 1988. *Island Boy.* New York: Viking.

COWLEY, JOY. 1981. *The Farm Concert.* Auckland, N.Z.: Shorthand.

———. 1981. *Stop.* Auckland, N.Z.: Shorthand.

DILLON, J. T. 1988. *Questioning and Teaching: A Manual for Practice.* London and Sydney: Croom Helm

DIXON, JOHN. 1967. *Growth Through English.* London: Oxford University Press.

DYSON, ANNE. 1987. "The Value of 'Time Off Task': Young Children's Spontaneous Talk and Deliberate Text." *Harvard Educational Review* 57:396–420.

EASTMAN, PHILLIP. 1961. *Go Dog Go.* New York: Random House.

EGAN, KIERAN. 1987. "Literacy and the Oral Foundations of Education." *Harvard Educational Review* 57:445–72.

GARDNER, HOWARD. 1978. *Developmental Psychology: An Introduction.* Boston: Little, Brown.

GIFF, PATRICIA. 1985. *In the Dinosaur's Paw.* New York: Dell.

———. 1985. *Lazy Lions and Lucky Lambs.* New York: Dell.

———. 1985. *Snaggle Doodle.* New York: Dell.

GOFFMAN, IRVING. 1976. "Replies and Responses." *Language in Society* 5:257–313.

———. 1961. *Asylums: Essays on the Social Situations of Mental Patients and Other Inmates.* New York: Anchor.

GOODLAD, JOHN. 1984. *A Place Called School.* New York: McGraw-Hill.

GORDON, SHARON. 1980. *The Easter Bunny's Lost Egg.* Mahwah, N.J.: Troll Associates.

GWYNNE, FRED. 1988. *The King Who Rained.* New York: Simon and Schuster.

HANDFORD, MARTIN. 1987. *Where's Waldo?* Boston: Little Brown.

HELLER, RUTH. 1981. *Chickens Aren't the Only Ones.* New York: Putnam.

HODGES, MARGARET. 1984. *St. George and the Dragon: A Golden Legend.* Adapted from Edmund Spencer's *Faire Queen,* illustrated by Trina Schart Hyman. Boston: Little, Brown.

HUCK, CHARLOTTE. 1989. *Princess Furball.* New York: Greenwillow Press.

JAMES, WILLIAM. [1900] 1958. *Talks to Teachers.* New York: Norton.

JOHNSON, CROCKETT. 1958. *The Blue Ribbon Puppies.* New York: Harper.

JOHNSON, ELIZABETH. 1957. *The Little Knight.* Boston: Little, Brown.

JOYCE, WILLIAM. 1990. *A Day with Wilbur Robinson.* New York: Harper and Row.

KARELITZ, ELLEN BLACKBURN. 1985. "Stories Never End." In *Breaking Ground: Teachers Relate Reading and Writing in Elementary Schools,* ed. Jane Hansen, Thomas Newkirk, and Donald Graves. Portsmouth, N.H.: Heinemann.

KEATS, EZRA JACK. 1987. *The Trip.* New York: Morrow.

———. 1976. *The Snowy Day.* New York: Scholastic.

KELLOGG, STEPHEN. 1988. *Johnny Appleseed.* New York: Morrow.

———. 1988. *Paul Bunyan.* New York: Morrow.

———. 1985. *Chicken Little.* New York: Morrow.

———. 1974. *The Mystery of the Missing Red Mitten.* New York: Dial.

———. 1971. *Can I Keep Him.* New York: Penguin.

KRAUS, ROBERT. 1989. *Phil the Ventriloquist.* New York: Greenwillow.

———. 1989. *How Spider Saved Santa Bug.* New York: Scholastic.

———. 1988. *How Spider Saved Easter.* New York: Scholastic.

KROLL, STEVEN. 1988. *Newsman Ned Meets the New Family.* New York: Scholastic.

LLOYD, D. 1984. *Thomas the Rabbit.* New York: Scholastic.

LURIE, ALISON. 1990. *Don't Tell the Grown-Ups: Subversive Children's Literature.* Boston: Little, Brown.

MARSHALL, JAMES. 1984. *George and Martha Back in Town.* Boston: Houghton Mifflin.

MAYHEW, KATHERINE, AND ANNA EDWARDS. [1936] 1966. *The Dewey School: The Laboratory School of the University of Chicago.* New York: Atherton.

MEHAN, HUGH. 1980. "The Competent Student." *Anthropology and Education Quarterly* 11:131–52.

———. 1979. *Learning Lessons: Social Organization in the Classroom.* Cambridge, Mass.: Harvard University Press.

MORROW, LESLEY MANDELL. 1988. "Young Children's Responses to One-to-One Story Readings in School Settings." *Reading Research Quarterly* 23:89–107.

MURRAY, DONALD. 1990. *Shoptalk.* Portsmouth, N.H.: Heinemann/ Boynton Cook.

NEWKIRK, THOMAS. 1989. *More than Stories: The Range of Children's Writing.* Portsmouth, N.H.: Heinemann.

NOBLE, TRINKA HAKES. 1980. *The Day Jimmy's Boa Ate the Wash.* New York: Dial.

NORTH, STEPHEN. 1987. *The Making of Knowledge in Composition.* Portsmouth, N.H.: Heinemann/Boynton Cook.

PALEY, VIVIAN. 1984. *Boys and Girls: Superheroes in the Doll Corner.* Chicago: University of Chicago Press.

———. 1981. *Wally's Stories.* Cambridge, Mass.: Harvard University Press.

PARISH, PEGGY. 1987. *Merry Christmas, Amelia Bedelia.* New York: Avon.

———. 1987. *Teach Us, Amelia Bedelia.* New York: Avon.

———. 1982. *Amelia Bedelia and the Baby.* New York: Avon.

PEARSON, DAVID, AND M. C. GALLAGHER. 1983. "The Instruction of Reading Comprehension." *Contemporary Educational Psychology* 8:317–44.

POLANYI, MICHAEL. 1962. *Personal Knowledge: Towards a Post-Critical Philosophy.* New York: Harper and Row.

RASKIN, ELLEN. 1968. *Spectacles.* New York: Atheneum.

SALINGER, J. D. 1951. *The Catcher in the Rye.* Boston: Little, Brown.

SCHON, DAVID. 1983. *The Reflective Practitioner: How Professionals Think in Action.* New York: Basic Books.

SEEGER, PETE. 1985. *Abiyoyo.* New York: Macmillan.

SENDAK, MAURICE. 1963. *Where the Wild Things Are.* New York: Harper and Row.

SILVERSTEIN, SHEL. 1981. "Gumeye Ball." In *A Light in the Attic.* New York: Harper and Row.

SMALL, DAVID. 1985. *Imogene's Antlers.* New York: Crown.

SOWERS, SUSAN. 1985. "Learning to Write in the Workshop: A Study of Grades One Through Four." In *Advances in Writing Research: Children's Early Writing Development,* ed. Marcia Farr. Norwood, N.J.: Ablex.

SPEARE, ELIZABETH. 1984. *The Sign of the Beaver*. New York: Dell.

SPIER, PETER. 1980. *People*. New York: Doubleday.

STEPIAN, JAN. 1988. *The Hungry Thing*. New York: Scholastic.

STEVENSON, JAMES. 1977. *Could Be Worse*. New York: Greenwillow.

TALLON, ROBERT. 1979. *Zoophabets*. New York: Scholastic.

THALER, MIKE. 1989. *The Teacher from the Black Lagoon*. New York: Scholastic.

THAYER, JANE. 1989. *The Popcorn Dragon*. New York: Morrow.

TOBIN, JOSEPH, DAVID WU, AND DANA DAVIDSON. 1989. *Preschool in Three Cultures: Japan, China, and the United States*. New Haven: Yale University Press.

VAN ALLSBURG, CHRIS. 1988. *Two Bad Ants*. Boston: Houghton Mifflin.

———. 1987. *The Z Was Zapped: A Play in Twenty-six Acts*. Boston: Houghton Mifflin.

———. 1985. *The Polar Express*. Boston: Houghton Mifflin.

VAN LEEUWEN, JEAN. 1983. *Tales of Oliver Pig*. New York: Dial.

VYGOTSKY, LEV. 1978. *Mind in Society: The Development of Higher Psychological Processes*. Cambridge, Mass.: Harvard University Press.

WABER, BERNARD. 1972. *Ira Sleeps Over*. Boston: Houghton Mifflin.

WEBER, ROSE-MARIE, AND MARY SHAKE. 1988. "Teachers' Rejoinders to Students' Responses in Reading Lessons." *Journal of Reading Behavior* 20:285–99.   LB1050 J62

WELLS, GORDON. 1985. *The Meaning Makers*. Portsmouth, N.H.: Heinemann.

WHITE, E. B. 1952. *Charlotte's Web*. New York: Harper and Row.

YORINKS, ARTHUR. 1988. *Company's Coming*. New York: Crown.